Wh[illegible]ou know about drink?

Dom Healy

Corron publishers

First published in Great Britain in 1998
by Corron Publishers
8 The Glade
Old Costessey
Norwich NR8 5EB

A CIP catalogue record for this book is available
from the British Library.

ISBN 0 9534049 0 0

Design, layout and Typesetting by Terry and Chris Marshall
Printed and bound in the UK by Page Bros (Norwich) Ltd

WHAT DO YOU KNOW ABOUT DRINK?

DOM HEALY

Acknowledgement

I would like to express my sincere thanks to David Bird, Muriel Wrigley, Chris and Terry Marshall and last but not least my wife Rita for their support and encouragement and without whose help it would not have been possible to produce this book.

Contents

Section 1

Introduction. 4

Map of wine growing areas. 6
Wine Production Chart. 8
Main wine growing countries. 9
Regions where most prolific grapes are grown. 24
Flavours and Aromas of Grape Varieties. 25
Other types of drink. 26
What do you know about drinks.
- General questions on wine. 39
- France. 55
- Italy. 56
- Germany. 57
- Spain/Portugal. 59
- Sparkling Wines. 60

True or False. 61
Health and Legal. 64
Drink Teasers. 67
Proverbs and Sayings. 85
Quotations. 87
Toasts. 89

Section 2

Brain Teasers. 91
Crosswords. 99
Map Teasers. 107
Wordsearch Teasers. 115

Section 3

Answers. 127
Glossary. 171

Introduction

Grape Variety

Good wine cannot be made from poor grapes. Different grape varieties will give different flavours and qualities to wines. The grape variety must be suitable for the growing area - some types are better suited to hot climates and others to temperate regions. Hot countries yield riper grapes which give greater flavour and higher levels of alcohol. Temperate countries produce lighter flavour wines and lower levels of alcohol.

Vineyard

The ideal location would be set on a hillside with the maximum of direct sunshine and good drainage. The tops of hillsides are much cooler and suffer from wind and lack of direct sunshine. At ground level wines receive less direct sunshine and can be prone to frosts and poor drainage.

Climate

Sunshine, rain, wind and temperature have an immense effect on the quality of the grape. Each of these elements interact to produce a good or poor quality crop of grapes. Climate can also vary from year to year which is an additional worry for the grower.

There are various types of soil i.e. chalk, slate, gravel, granite, etc. which will determine the type of wine to be grown. The best soil is one with good natural drainage.

Viticulture

Method of growing the vine.

Vinification

Term used for all the operations and processes which turn grapes into wine.

Vigneron

The vigneron's skill is vital for the making and maturing of the wine. These start with the harvesting - timing is very important, the grapes can be picked all at once or in batches when the grapes have achieved the desired ripeness.

This is followed by the sorting and pressing of the grapes, the fermentation of the juice must be controlled with great skill and knowledge. After fermentation the wine is put into casks where it is matured until it achieves the quality desired by the vigneron.

Foreword

Wine is a fascinating subject. With the world's consumption of wine increasing annually not only are people drinking more wine but their tastes are changing. To produce quality wine at a reasonable price is one of the main objectives of wine producers. Wine is to be enjoyed, even at wine tastings your opinion and perception is a very personal thing, each of us will have different reactions to sensations we experience through our eyes, nose and palate. Some people are intimidated by the mystique of wine, the jargon, the rituals, the so called commandments associated with the subject. Of course there are people who are wine experts - Masters of Wine, of which there are few, and people in the trade - but we can't all be like one of them unless we decide to make a career for ourselves in the wine trade. This book will enable the reader to learn about wine and matters connected with all types of drink in a fun, light-hearted way. It is designed to reassure the beginner that it is possible to enjoy the subject without knowing the jargon.

There are over 2000 questions and brain teasers to solve and as you solve them you will learn the story of vine to wine and much more. In this book I have tried to share my pleasure in appreciating wine, I hope you will also enjoy the experience and find the book a useful and helpful guide.

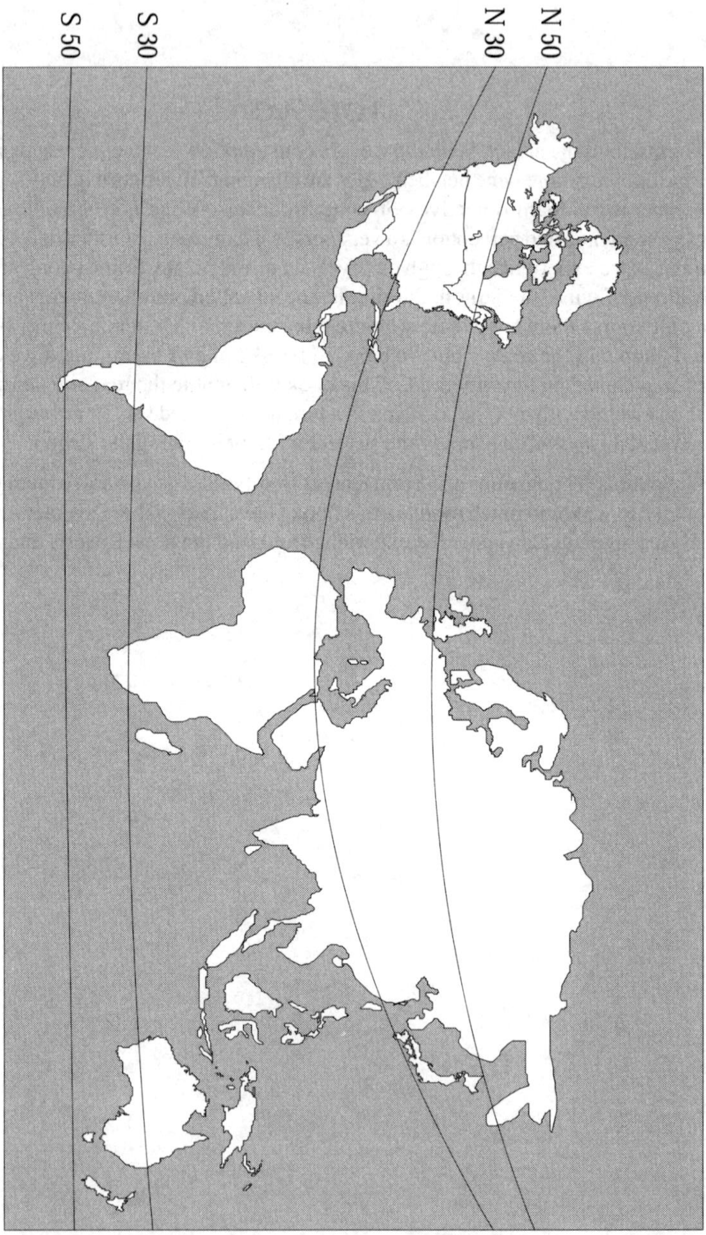

The World's wine producing countries are located between the latitudes 30 N and 50 N in the northern hemisphere and between 30 S and 50 S in the southern hemisphere. Europe produces 4/5 of the world's wine.

A YEAR IN THE VINEYARD (NORTHERN HEMISPHERE)

THE VINE		THE VINE GROWER
Dormant	January	Miscellaneous maintenance. Stakes and wires repaired.
Dormant	February	Pruning and fertilizing.
Sap rises	March	Weeding, grafting. Vines cleaned and trained.
Buds appear	April	Ploughing back to aerate soil.
Leaf growth	May	Vine shoots attached. Application of weed-killer
Flowering	June	Vine shoots clipped. Tying up and tying down of branches.
Grapes form	July	Chemical spraying. Ends of leafy branches pruned.
Development of bunches	August	General maintenance. Preparation of equipment for harvesting.
Grapes ripen	September	Harvesting.
End of Harvest	October	Vinification. Trench ploughing. Preparation of soil for replanting.
Dormant	November	Soil replacement. Burning branches. Frost protection of vines.
Dormant	December	Pruning and fertilizing.

Wine production

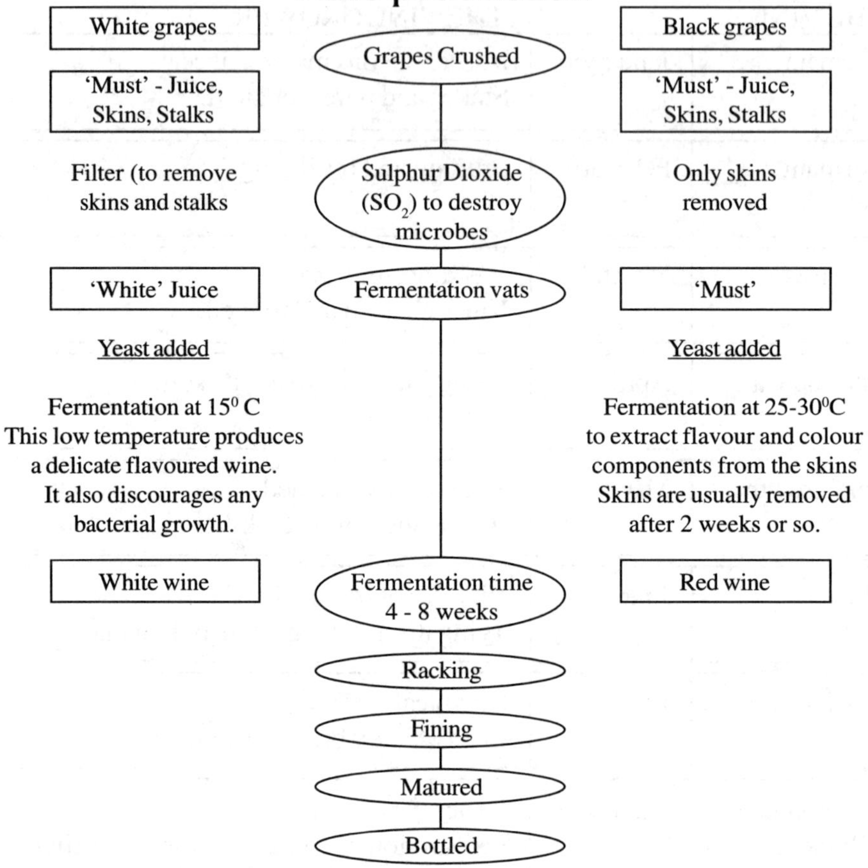

Fermentation ends when all the sugar has been consumed by the yeast.

The dead yeast forms a sediment know as 'LEES' at the bottom of the tank.

The wine is removed without disturbing the lees over a period, this process is known as racking.

The wine will then go through a process known as fining which removes any impurities (similar to clarifying a consommé soup using egg whites).

Substances used to clarify wine are coagulants such as fish glue, egg whites, gelatin, ox blood, casein and the most widely used bentonite (a powdery earth).

The wine is then matured following clarification to develop flavour.

Barrels are topped up when evaporation or absorption takes place as wine deteriorates when left in contact with air.

When the wine is bottled further flavour development can take place.

Wine Growing Countries

France

Alsace

A land with a very disturbed history: was German up to late 17th century, became part of France after 30 Years War, back to Germany in 1870 after Franco-Prussian war, finally reverting to France in 1918. The most beautiful vineyard area of France, specialising also in haute-cuisine and eaux-de-vie. Divided between the two departments of Haut-Rhin and Bas-Rhin, the former producing the better wines.

Climate: Vineyards are all situated on eastern slopes of Vosges mountains and lie in the rain shadow. Thus long sunny summers and low rainfall. The higher the mountain, the drier the climate; thus, the southern sector is the best. Significant factor in wine quality.

Soil: Less significant. Varied, but mainly rich alluvial mixture of limestone and silica overlaid with loess.

Vines: Riesling - the finest, giving wines that are dry, firm and with great elegance.

Gewürztraminer - a very pronounced spicy bouquet, with lower acidity. The most individual tasting white wine of France.

Muscat - a dry wine with pronounced spicy bouquet; frequently used as an aperitif.

Sylvaner - the most widely grown grape, giving a somewhat dull earthy wine.

Pinot Gris - used to be known as Tokay d'Alsace, full-bodied and very fine.

Wines: Unusually, for France, named after grape variety. Mostly vinified dry, firm and with around 11% alcohol. German system of late picking also used, producing wines of great richness, but German names must not be used e.g. not spatlese, but 'vendange tardive' and 'selection de grains nobles'. Wine from blend of grape varieties is Edelzwicker. Few wines, some from single vineyard (with exception of the most favoured sites) and are bought under name of grape variety and negociant.

AOC Laws: Granted in 1962. The simplest in France - AC Alsace and AC Alsace Grand Cru with minimum alcohols of 8.5% and 11% respectively. (Grand Cru has not yet been used, due to inter-professional squabbling!) All wine must be bottled in Alsace (1972) in the flute d'Alsace. A few of the most favoured sites are occasionally named on the label.

Good Houses: Trimbach, Hugel, Dopff and Irion, Kuentz-Bas, Schlumberger, Gisselbrecht, Kuenn, Beyer, Dopff au Moulin.

Bordeaux

Most important wine region of France, producing 2.5 million hectolitres each year from 240,000 hectoacres of vineyard, comprising one-eighth of the region's land surface. Great range of wines, from dry white to sweet white and light reds to very tannic reds.

Climate: temperate, maritime, high humidity due to proximity of sea and rivers.

Soil: Médoc and Graves - gravel
St. Émilion - hills clay with limestone subsoil
Sauternes - gravel over chalk and clay subsoil.

Vines: black - cabernet sauvignon
cabernet franc
merlot
malbec and petit verdot (lesser importance)

white - sauvignon
semillon
muscadelle

Training: mainly Guyot simple and Guyot double

Principal Districts

Médoc — 99.5% red. Famous communes of St. Estèphe, Pauillac, St. Julien, Margaux. High proportion of cabernet sauvignon used. Châteaux classified in 1855.

Graves — Red and dry white. Château Haut-Brion.

Sauternes — Sweet white. Semillon grape affected by pourriture noble (noble rot). Château d'Yquem.

Premières Côtes de Bordeaux — Less sweet white wines.

Entre-Deux-Mers — Large quantity of average quality dry white. Mostly cooperatives.

St. Émilion — Red, fullest and heartiest of Bordeaux. Easily confused with Burgundy. Merlot predominates. Less tannin, earlier maturing. Château Cheval-Blanc, Château Ausane.

Pomerol — Similar to St. Emilion. Chateau Pétrus.

Bourg, Blaye — Red and white of lesser quality.

Burgundy

A relatively small region, producing wines of supremely high quality, and thus commanding a very high price. The reds have less tannin than Bordeaux, due to the less tannic grape and shorter fermentation on the skins, and thus they mature earlier and have a shorter life. The whites are the finest of all dry whites, full-bodied, rich and spicy.

Climate: Pattern similar to Bordeaux, but with continental influence. The northernmost area in world producing great red wine. Nothing unique which could explain excellence of wine.

Soil: Côte d'Or is edge of plateau of various sandy limestones, weathered by erosion and cultivation into limey clay soil. Outcrops of limestone perfect for white production. Beaujolais is granite-based.

Vines: Black - Pinot Noir (Côte d'Or & Macon).
Gamay (Beaujolais & Macon)
White - Chardonnay (for all quality wines) & Aligote

Training: Côte d'Or - Guyot Simple; Beaujolais - Gobelet

Principal Districts

Côte d'Or: Irregular escarpment 30 miles long, varying in width from one and a half miles to a few hundred yards.

Côte de Nuits:- all red with medium tannin and long life: Gevrey-Chambertin, Morey-St-Denis, Chambolle-Musigny, Vougeot, Vosne-Romanee, Nuits-St-Georges.

Côte de Beaune: Reds softer and lighter in style: Aloxe-Corton, Beaune, Pommard, Volnay. Whites: Corton-Charlemagne, Meursault, Puligny-Montrachet.

Côte Chalonnaise: Continuation of Côte d'Or, but deteriorated into jumble of hillocks. Best can reach standard of average Côte de Beaune. Major communes: Rully (white & sparkling), Mercurey (red), Givry (white), Montagny (white).

Maconnais: Generally undistinguished, producing Macon Rouge and Macon Blanc. Best district is round Pouilly and Fuissé. These wines can be really memorable.

Beaujolais: Contiguous with Maconnais. Mainly granite hills. Northern part, consisting of 35 villages, is best. These can bottle wine as Beaujolais Villages. 9 can use own name (the Grands Crus):- Julienas, St-Amour, Chenas, Moulin-a-Vent, Fleurie, Chiroubles, Morgan, Brouilly & Côte-de-Brouilly.

Chablis: Lying to the NW of Côte d'Or. Chalky clay soil. All white and can be very fine indeed. Lighter and crisper.

Buying Burgundy

Burgundy vineyards greatly subdivided due to Code Napoleon e.g. Clos de Vougeot has 80 owners, all making their own style of wine of Bordeaux, where each vineyard has one owner. Thus, name of negociant (person who buys and blends wine) is more important than name of vineyard. Also, avoid confusing Grand Cru vineyard name with that of a mere village, e.g. Chevalier-Montrachet and Puligny-Montrachet.

Champagne

History: Centred on Reims and Epernay. An area of great antiquity for vine growing. Originally still wines, and rivals to Burgundy. Dom Pérignon cellarmaster of Benedictine abbey of Hautvillers around 1700 realised that, by using thicker bottles and tying down stopper with string, the sparkle could be retained. Pioneered blending. Madame Cliquot invented remuage. Name jealously guarded.

Climate: The most northerly AC region of France, resulting in delicate nature of Champagne.

Soil: Kimmeridge clay (as in Chablis).

Districts: Main four: Montagne de Reims, Vallee de la Marne, Côte des Blancs, Aube. Each individual village has quality rating, dependent on price paid for grapes.

Important 100% villages: Ambonnay, Ay, Bouzy, Mailly, Sillery, Verzenay, Avize, Cramant.

Viticulture: Pinot Noir, Pinot Meunier, Chardonnay. Gamay eliminated from Aube.
Training mostly chablis or guyot. Soil lifted back up slopes every three years.

Vinification: Most grapes are sold to champagne houses.
Traditional press holds 4 tonnes grapes.

Four pressings:		
	vin de cuvée	2,000 litres
	premièr taille) deuxierne taille)	600 litres
	rebeche	not allowed

Sulphuring and débourbage
Racking and assemblage - blending wines of one village.
Coupage - making final blend
Bottling - addition of yeast - liqueur de tirage
Maturation "sur lattes" NV minimum 1 year
V minimum 3 years
Remuage - "riddling" and storage "sur pointes"
Degorgement Dosage addition of liqueur d'expedition
Corking and muzzling with muselets.

Côteaux Champenois - still Champagne - can be white, rosé (Rosé de Riceys) or red (Bouzy Rouge).

Champagne Houses

Ayala
Barancourt
Besserat de Bellfon
Billecart-Salmon
Bollinger
Canard-Duchêne's
Charles and Pieur
Charles Heidsieck/Henriot
Heidsieck-Monopola
Jacquesson
Joseph Perrier
Krug
Lanson
Laurent-Perrier
Louis Roederer
Marne et Champagne
Mercier
Moet et Chandon
Mumm
Piper Heidsieck
Pol Roger
Pommery and Greno
Ruinart
Salon Tatinger-Irroy
Veuve Clicquot-Ponsardin

The Loire Valley

Longest river in France - over 600 miles.

Climate: northerly, mild, similar to southern England, except that total hours of sunshine is greater. Therefore best suited to white production.

Soil: mostly clay over chalk; sand and gravel in Chinon/Bourgueil.

Principal districts: Pays Nantais
Anjou - Saumur
Touraine
Central Vineyards

<u>Pays Nantais</u>

Vines: Muscadet (AOC) and gros plant (VDQS)

Pruning: Guyot simple

Notable wines: Muscadet de Sevre et Maine

<u>Anjou Saumur</u>

Vines: red - cabernet france, cabernet sauvignon
rosé - cabernet, groslot
white - chenin only

Pruning: Guyot simple and Lenz Moser

Notable wines: Côteaux du Layon (sweet), Saumur (still, sparkling and red), Rosé d'Anjou

<u>Touraine</u>

Vines: red - cabernet franc
white - chenin

Pruning: gobelet

Notable wines: Best Loire reds - Chinon and Bourgueil. White - Vouvray, still and sparkling

<u>Central Vineyards</u>

Vines: White predominantly - sauvignon, chasselas
Red - pinot noir

Pruning: Guyot simple

Notable wines: Pouilly-Fumé, Sancerre

The Rhône Valley

The best of southern viticulture, contrasting with the Loire Valley, the best of northern viticulture. Mostly red (cf.Loire, mostly white). Need time to mature - 10 years or more. Two basic sub-divisions: northern sector and southern sector.

Climate: Mild winters, long hot summers.

Pruning: Principally some form of gobelet or bush type. Supporting stakes needed in northern sector as protection against Mistral.

Principal Districts

Northern Sector

Côte Rôtie
Soil - clay and chalk on steep slopes
Vines - Syrah (black) and Viognier (white)
Wine - red, delicate, possibly finest of all Rhône

Condrieu
Soil - granite, very steep terraces
Vines - Viognier
Wine - delicate and flowery. Best of Rhône whites

Château-Grillet A superior Condrieu. Smallest vineyard with own appellation

Hermitage
Soil - a prominent granite hill
Vines - Syrah (black), Marsanne (white), Roussanne (white).,
Wines - red and white, robust and full-flavoured.

Crozes-Hermitage (red and white)

St. Joseph (red and white)

Cornas (red)

St Péray (white and sparkling)

B. Southern Sector

Châteauneuf-du-Pape First AC district in France, granted 1923

Soil - enormous stones, overlying clay
Vines - 13 varieties
Wines - rich, smooth and strong (minimum 12.5%, highest in France). 98% red.

Tavel
Soil - 3 types: stones over clay, sandy, calcareous
Vines - Grenache, Cinsault and 8 others
Wine - best rosé of France, dry and full.

Beaumes-de-Venise (sweet white muscat)

Gigondas (red)

Côtes du Rhône Villages

Côtes du Rhône

Lesser Districts of France

The Midi

The vineyards of the Midi stretch from the Rhône estuary to the Spanish border and from the Mediterranean Sea to the foothills of the Central Massi. More than one third of the total French wine comes from the Midi. Red - White - Rosé are made.

Quality: Vin de Table - AOC

Red wines are better quality. White wines lack acidity and fruit.

Regions: Languedoc-Roussilon, Fitou, Minervois, Corbieres, Côte du Luberon.

Blanquette de Limoux is a good quality sparkling wine made by the Champagne method.

Corsica

Wines high in alcohol with the Rosés being best.

Cahors

South west France dark red wine. Obtained AOC status in 1971.

Bergerac

Good quality wines produced in this area East of Bordeaux. White wines sold under name of Montravel and Monbazillac. Red wine as Bergerac Rouge.

Gaillac

Situated north east of Toulouse. Red, white and rosé and sparkling wines are produced.

Savoie

Area: Lake Geneva down to Aix-les-Bains and Cambery

Grape Varieties: Mainly Jacquere - Altesse for white wines. Gamay-Mondeus for red wines.

Best Wines: Crepy (A.C) Seyssel and Apremint (V.D.Q.S.)

Jura

Area: East of Burgundy. A.C. wines red - white - rosé and Vin Jaunes.
(Vin Jaunes = Yellow wines)
(Vin de Pailles = Straw wines)

For sweet wines the grapes are dried on straw.
Red wines have a brownish "onion skin" tinge.
Rosés are similar but paler and usually dry.
Best Rosé is Rosé D'Arbois. Only second to Tavel Rosé.
Best wine is Château Chalon (like a dry Sherry six years under a layer or flor, it is sold in 50cl bottles called Clavelin).

Italy

Almost one vast vineyard! Equal to France as the world's largest producer. Over 90% is low quality table wine, but many fine wines are produced in the northern half.

Climate: Too hot in south for quality wine production. Even in north, hilly districts are favoured for quality.

Controls: DOC system introduced in 1963. More stringent but less effective than French AC system. Three levels -

1. Vino da tavola (table wine)
2. Denominazions di origine controllata, DOC
3. Denominazione di origine controllata e garantita, DOCG

Wine names: Mostly named after village, eg. Barolo, Valpolicella, Orvieto. Sometimes grape name is used, but this must always be accompanied by name of village, eg. Barbera d'Asti, Verdicchio dei Castelli de Jesi. A few have special wine name, eg. Chianti.

Principal Wines

Barolo DOCG — Arguably Italy's greatest wine; big, dark and tannic. Made from nebbiolo. Needs long maturation.

Barbaresco DOCG — Lighter version of Barolo, and from a neighbouring village.

Asti Spumante DOC — Sparkling wine made from moscato grapes. Sweet; made by method of interrupted fermentation.

Barbera d'Asti DOC — Made from Barbera grapes. Dark ruby and of no great aspirations to quality.

Valpolicella DOC — The Beaujolais of Italy. Bright red, youthful and fruity.
Recioto della Valpolicella is a sweet and velvety red wine made from over-ripe grapes from the top of the bunches. The Amarone version is a dry, and highly alcoholic, version. Delicious!

Lambrusco DOC — A semi-sparkling (frizzante) red wine, often semi-sweet. Very popular in USA.

Chianti DOCG — A red wine made from sangiovese and canaiolo grapes (black), with some trebbiano and malvasia (white). Must from dried grapes added after racking, to give freshness and a slight 'prickle' (the governo process). Ordinary chianti known as chianti putto. Chianti classico is made in the better quality inner zone. A wine with a higher alcohol is known as superiore. Wines aged longer in cask are riserva.

Verdicchio DOC — A delicate dry white wine made from verdicchio grapes. Best village is Castelli di Jesi.

Orvieto DOC — A white wine traditionally made dry (secco) or medium sweet (abbocato).

Soave - DOC	Probably the best white wine of Italy. Being made in the north, it has more acidity than many of the other wines.
Frascati - DOC	A dry white wine, somewhat dull.
Marsala - DOC	A fortified wine made in Sicily. Usually dark and sweet. Essential for the making of zabaglione.
Sassicaia - DOC	The best red wine of Italy, did not become a DOC until 1994 because it is made from cabernet sauvignon, which was not allowed until then.

Germany

A comparatively small region in the area of the river Rhine and its tributaries, and situated near the northern limit of wine production. Tenth in the world league of wine production, although the yield per unit area is very high (200hl/ha). 85% white. UK biggest customer.

Climate: Most northerly in Europe and vine has to struggle for survival. Micro-climate becomes important, as maximum benefit has to be gained from weak sun.

Vines: Riesling - supreme quality, but low yield

Silvaner - softer and milder, double yield

Muller-Thurgau - one of the many crosses between Riesling and Silvaner

Principal Regions

Mosel-Saar-Ruwer: Slate soil on very steep slopes, only those facing south or south-east. 65% Riesling. Wines flowery and with crisp acidity.

Rheingau: South-facing slopes, sheltered by Taunus mountains.
Quartzite soil. 76% Riesling. Finest of all German wines, elegant, balanced and full.

Rheinhessen: Large and productive region. Milder climate.
Soil loam and red sandstone. 36% Muller-Thurgau, 28% Silvaner. Wines mild and fruity, yet elegant.

Rheinpfalz: (Palatinate) Sunniest and driest region. Various soils.
24% Muller-Thurgau, 23% Silvaner. Wines bigger and fatter, with lower acidity, "Palatinate clod-hoppers".

1971 Wine Law divided German wines into three principal categories:

1 Table wine (Deutscher Tafelwein)
2 Quality wine (Qualitatswein bestimmten Anbaugebiete, QbA)
3 Quality wine with special attributes (Qualitatswein mit Pradikat, QmP)

The attributes being:
- Kabinett (above average quality)
- Spatlese (late gathered)
- Auslese (selected ripe bunches)
- Beerenauslese (selected ripe berries)
- Trockenbeerenauslese (selected berries with Edelfaule or Noble Rot)

Table wine regions: Mosel, Rhein, Main, Neckar, Ober-Rhein.

Quality wine regions: Ahr, Mosel-Saar-Ruwer, Mittelrhein, Nahe, Rheingau, Rheinhessen, Rheinpfalz, Franken, Hessische Bergstrasse, Wurttemberg, Baden.

Smallest unit is an individual vineyard (Einzellage). A group of similar neighbouring vineyards is a Grosslage and a group of Grosslagen forms a Bereich.

Iberian Peninsular

Spain

Third largest production in the world - mostly table wine. Much is of rather poor quality, but some is excellent. Consejo Regulador administers regulations for quality wines, the Denominacion de Origen, similar to but less stringent than the French AOC regulations.

Climate: Continental and harsh, with dry, torrid summers and biting winters. Andalusia is much milder, being tempered by Mediterranean. Quality regions all at high altitude or associated with rivers.

Vines:

Black -
- Garnacha (high yield)
- Tempranillo (colour & body, but little flavour)
- Graciano (marked perfume)
- Mazuelo (susceptible to oideum).
- Tinto fino, tinto basto etc. etc.

White -
- Garnacha blanca (alcohol and acidity)
- Viura (flavour)
- Malvasia (flavour)
- Parellada (light, elegant style)
- Macabeo etc. etc.

Principal Denominacions

Valdepeñas: (La Nabcha) The land of Don Qioxote, producing greatest quantity in Spain, mostly low quality and destined for carafes of Madrid's cafes.

Rioja: DO Upland region along banks of Rio Ebro and Rio Oja. Divided into three districts: Rioja Alta (best & highest), Rioja Alavesa (also good wines, but bigger), Rioja Baja (lower altitude, coarser wines). Best wines of Spain, matured for long period in oak. Little variation from year to year, thus vintages not important. Red produced from garnacha, tempranillo, graciano and maxuela; whites from viura, malvasia and garnacha blanco.

Penedés: DO Coastal area with vines growing high on sides of mountain. Large production of sparkling wine from parellada grapes, around Villafranca del Penedés. Torres family produces many fine wines from classic French grapes.

Tarragona: Used to be famous for a coarse, strong, sweet red wine (Red Biddy). Now produces large volume of red and white table wine.

Navarra: DO Region to the north of Rioja. Produces good quality red and white wines.

La Mancha: DO Vast arid region south of Madrid. Extreme climate very hot in summer and very cold in winter. Largest producer of wines in Spain.

Valencia: DO Lies east of La Mancha. Produces red, white and rosé wines.

Portugal

Eighth in world production league. Regulations administered by Junta Nacional do Vinho. All exporters must belong to Gremio do Comercio de Exportacao de Vinhos, which issues certificates of origin. Control very thorough. Virtually all produced north of river Tejo.

Climate: Northern half ideal for grapes - ample rain (except in Upper Douro) and a long bright, rather than blazing summer.

Vines: Tourigo, mourisco, tinta pinheira, etc. etc.

Principal Denominacáo do Origem Controlada (D.O.C.)

Vinhos Verdes: NW Portugal, between Douro and Minho. Mixed cultivation. Vines grown on pergolas, fences, up trees. Grapes picked early and not always ripe, hence wine is very youthful and 'green'. High acidity and low alcohol. Slight sparkle supposed to be malolactic fermentation, but actually carbon dioxide is injected.

Dáo: Strong wines of high alcohol, mostly red and very smooth, due to high concentration of glycerine. Soil decomposed granite & schist.

Other notable wines - Colares, Carcavelos, Bucelas, Moscatel de Setubal

The New World

California

Rapidly challenging France as the source of the world's finest wines: climate, soil and other conditions are conducive to production of good wine. 70% of wine sales in US are from California. Production roughly equals AOC wines of France.

History: Started by Cortez in 1524. Continued by missions until 1830, using Mission grape. 1861 Colonel Haraszthy planted cuttings from Europe.

Regions: North Coast, Sacramento, Central, San Joaquin Valley, South Coast.

Districts: North Coast produces best wines - Napa, Sonoma, Mendocino, Livermore, Santa Clara, San Benito, Santa Cruz, Monterey.

Wines: All named after grape varieties:-
Red - Cabernet Sauvignon, Pinot Noir, Zinfandel
White - Chardonnay, Sauvignon Blanc (Blanc Fumé), Semillon, Johannisberger Riesling, Traminer

Vineyards: Beaulieu, Beringer, Robert Mondavi, Christian Brothers, Sterling, Joseph Heitz, Sonoma, Concannon, Wente, Paul Masson, Dry Creek.

South Africa

Although producing wine for 300 years, only just learning to cope with dry, hot climate, (although reliable). Now producing excellent sherries and table wines.

History: 1654 first cuttings arrived from Holland. First fine wine made at Groot Constantia in 1679. KWV formed in 1918 and fixes minimum price for distillation.

Areas: Best for table wines: - Constantia, Durbanville, Stellenbosch, Paarl, Tulbagh, Malmesbury, Worcester.

Wines: Named after estate and vine variety.
Red - Cabernet Sauvignon, Cinsault, Shiraz, Pinotage
White - Chenin Blanc (Steen), Riesling, Traminer

Laws: Very well ordered. Wines of Origin 1973. Neck label states:-
Blue band - specified area (or estate)
Red band - vintage
Green band - vine variety
Superior Quality

Australia

As with California, conditions very congenial for vine-growing. Very modern technology. Beginning to produce high-quality wines of elegance and lightweight. Best areas are between the 38th and 34th parallels - other areas are too hot and dry for wine production. Australia is now the 4th largest supplier to the UK after France, Germany and Italy.

History:	Captain Arthur Phillip landed in 1788 and included vines in his cargo. Early wines were of export "burgundy" type. Continued up to 1925.
Regions:	NSW - Hunter River Valley, Murrumbidgee Irrigation Area Victoria - Mildura, Tahbilk, Rutherglen, Great Western South Australia - Barossa Valley, Coonawarra, Clare Western Australia - Swan Valley
Wines:	Named after vine varieties, although European imitation names still linger. Red - Cabernet Sauvignon, Pinot Noir, Merlot, Shiraz White - Rhine Riesling, Traminer, Chenin Blanc.

Austria

Most of the vineyards are in eastern Austria near Vienna. The majority of Austrian wine is white. A good deal of this white wine is made from the Veltliner grape. Because Austria has an ideal climate for wine making - long hot Summers, cold dry Winters and a mild Autumn - plus rich soils about 200 grape varieties can be grown.

Like the French, Germans and Italians the Austrians have strict categories of the quality of their wines, decided by the must weight (or sugar level) of the wine.

Kabinett - Spaetlese - Auslese - Beerenauslese - Trockenbeerenauslese

Greece

RETSINA is a dry to medium dry white wine to which pine essence has been added.
DEMESTICA is the most well known Greek branded wine. It may be red or white.

Hungary

Hungary makes large quantities of sound quality red and white wines which come from five regions, Great Plains, Southern Trans Danube and Northern Trans Danube being most famous. Lake Belaton divides north from south and this area has the longest hours of sunshine in Europe. On the eastern side of the lake Egar produces BULLS BLOOD, the wine may be made in 17 villages around the town. It is a full bodied dry red wine. EGRI BIKAVER
Tokay is the name of a town as well as a wine. The grapes in this region are left on the vines into the late autumn to develop Noble Rot thus making a luscious, sweet golden coloured wine.
TOKAY ASZU

Bulgaria

The Bulgarian climate is perfect for vine growing. Within the country each wine growing area has its own individual climate which helps to determine the character or style of the different type of wine produced there.
In the northern regions between the Balkan and the Danube the grey forest soil produces rich vineyards and a bounty of red and white wine. Cabernet and the Gamza are supreme examples of the superb red wines available, while among the whites, Riesling, Pinot, Chardonnay and Sauvignon Blanc stand shoulder to shoulder with them. They are all distinguished by their fruitiness, their pronounced bouquet and their strength of character.

In the south in the valleys which reach their way between the mountains, the dark black soil yields heavy harvests of those grapes which produce deep and full-bodied wine. Mavrud and Merlot are distinguished by their full-bodied softness and lower acidity. Throughout Bulgaria there are over 130 wineries. On four of these has now been conferred the title Centre of Excellence, Suhindol, Sumen, Assenorgrad and Khan Krum have been so honoured. All wines selected for export to the U.K. market from above.

Chile

Chile's wine growing areas are cradled between the Pacific's coastal mountain range and the Andes. To the north are vast deserts and in the south, the snows or Antarctica. Natural barriers which probably saved Chile from the scourge of Phylloxera.

Most of the wines which Chile exports are made from Cabernet Sauvignon, Cabernet Franc, Merlot, Pinot, Cot and Verdot (red wines) and Sauvignon Blanc, Semillon, Riesling and Chardonnay (white wines).

Almost all of these noble varieties are grown in Chile's so called Central Valley. This really is not a valley at all but a large plateau in the centre of the country at some 600 metres above sea level. Within the central valley three main wine growing regions are distinguished Maipo, Rapel and Maule.

The vineyards lie in the middle over latitudes 27 and 39. A length of some l450KMs producing a vast range of quality wine.

Other wine producing countries

These include Argentina, New Zealand, Romania, Former Czechoslovakia, Old Russian Empire, Former Yugoslavia, etc.

Regions where most prolific grape varieties are grown

Black Grapes

CABERNET SAUVIGNON	World Wide use but famous in Bordeaux and SW France.
MERLOT	As above
CABERNET FRANC	Loire Valley, Bordeaux, Northern Italy, New World.
SYRAH	S. Rhône Valley, SW France, Australia (known as Shiraz) New World.
PINOT NOIR	Burgundy, S Africa, Spain, USA especially Washington State, Australia, Hungary.
GAMAY	Beaujolais, Burgundy, Loire.
GRENACHE	S. Rhône, S. France, Loire.
NEBBIOLO	Italy, especially in the North, California.
ZINFANDEL	California
SANGIOVESE	Northern Italy - (Chianti).
TEMPRANILLO	Spain, especially Rioja and Portugal.
CARIGNAN	France, Spain, California
VIOGNIER	Rhône Valley - (Condrieu)
CINSAULT	SW France, Corsica, S. Africa, Lebanon, Algeria.

White Grapes

CHARDONNAY	World Wide (used for Champagne/Chablis).
SAUVIGNON BLANC	Bordeaux, Loire, Australia, S. Africa, New Zealand, Chile, California.
SEMILLON	Bordeaux, Hungary, USA, Australia, Chile, New Zealand, Argentina.
RIESLING	Germany, Alsace, Austria, N. Italy, USA, Australia, New Zealand, S. Africa, E. Europe, S. America.
MULLER-THURGAU	Germany, N. Italy, Australia, Czechoslovakia, New Zealand, USA.
GEWÜRZTRAMINER	Alsace, N. Italy, Australia, E. Europe, New Zealand, Chile, California.
ALIGOTE	Burgundy, E. Europe.
CHENIN BLANC	Loire, USA, Australia, S. France, S. Africa, New Zealand.
PINOT NOIR	Champagne, Alsace, N. Italy, Germany, E. Europe, California.
SYLVANER	Germany, Alsace, Austria.
COLUMBARD	SW France, California
MUSCAT	S. France, Italy, Alsace, New World.

Flavours and aromas of grape varieties

Black Grapes

CABERNET FRANC	Raspberries, Liquorice, Violet, Blackcurrants, Herbs.
CABERNET SAUVIGNON	Blackcurrants, Pencil Shavings, Tobacco, Mint, Cigar Boxes, Toffeeish.
CARIGNAN	Hot Berries, Tar.
CINSAULT	Dried Fruit, Floral Aromas.
GAMAY	Cherries, Strawberries, Black Pepper, Boiled Sweets (Drink Young).
GRENACHE	Berry Fruits.
MERLOT	Plums, Toffee, Grassy Aroma, Truffle, (Drink Young).
NEBBIOLO	Black Cherries, Chocolate, Tar, Prunes, Tobacco.
PINOT NOIR	Strawberries, Raspberries, Chocolatey, Compost.
SANGIOVESE	Cherries, Plums, Raisins, Cedar, Tobacco, Perfume.
SYRAH	Blackberries, Blueberries, Tar, Herbs, Black Pepper, Leather, Creosote, Black Treacle, Liquorice.
TEMPRANILLO	Strawberries, Cherries, Spice, Vanilla, Oak.
ZINFANDEL	Blackberries, Cherries, Spicy, Herbs, Black Pepper.

White Grapes

CHARDONNAY	Buttery, Honey, Pineapple, Nutty, Ripe Fruit, Toast, Melon.
SAUVIGNON BLANC	Greenish, Gooseberry, Lemon, Honey, Oaky, Cut Grass, Cats Pee.
SEMILLON	Buttery, Flinty, Greenish, Honey, Lemon.
RIESLING	Grape, Apple, Honey, Spicy, Lemon, Petrol.
MULLER-THURGAU	Flowery, Cats Pee, Mango.
GEWURZTRAMINER	Perfumed Violets, Lychees, Spicy.
CHENNIN BLANC	Acidic, Apple, Apricot, Wet Straw, Lemon, Honey.
PINOT BLANC	Nutty, Citrus Fruits.
SYLVANER	Acidic, Fruity, Faintly Scented.
MUSCAT	Perfumed, Grapey flavour, Elderberries, (Drink Young).
COLUMBARD	Flowery, Citrus, Green Apples, (Drink young).

Other Types of Drinks

Sherry

History: Xeres founded by Phoenicians 1100BC. Taken by Greeks 450 BC, Romans 205BC, Barbarian Vandals AD409 (hence Analusia), Visigoths, then Moors from Africa AD 711. In AD 1251, Moorish King of Jerez surrendered to Christian Ferdinand III. Jerez remained on frontier between Moors and Christians, hence the name Jerez de la Frontera.

Climate: Very hot summers. Rainfall 50cm (20") per year. Predominant winds from the sea. Hot dry Levante wind.

Soils: Albariza - white; up to 80% chalk; best wines, lowest yield.
Barro - darker brown; less than 30% chalk; poorer wines.
Arena - sand mixed with clay; poorest wines; highest yield, more than twice that of albariza. Best zones known as Jerez Superior. Pagos.

Vines: Palomino - tasty and sweet with high sugar content grown on albarizas for best finos.
Pedro Ximénez - golden coloured and even sweeter; used for making the best quality sweeting wine.
Moscatel Gordo Blanco - used for lesser quality sweetening wine.

Vinification: Grapes pressed in horizontal press. Fermentation in temperature - controlled stainless steel vats. Acidity increased if necessary by adding tartaric acid. Natural alcohol 9 - 12%. Fermented out to dryness. All sherry is naturally dry.

Classification: First done December/January before racking.
/ = una raya (fino)
// = dos rayas (oloroso)
/. = raya y punto (uncertain)
= distillation

Fortification: Finos taken up to only 15.5% vol, to preserve flor. Olorosos to 18% vol, to destroy flor. Wines are kept as anadas (wines of the year).

Solera System: Following June, anada wines classified again, then entered into youngest criadera. System consists of rows of butts, each containing successively older wine. Can have up to 12 'scales' or rows. Oldest row from which wine is extracted for shipping is the 'solera'; youngest row is '12th criadera'. The solera is topped up from 1st criadera, which in turn is topped up from 2nd criadera etc.. Not more than one third may be taken out of a butt at any one time, but may be done several times a year.

Blending: All commercial sherries are blended to individual recipes. They contain standard amounts of:
old wines (for flavour - expensive)
rayas (coarser cheaper wines)
dulce (sweeting wines from PX or moscatel)
vino de color (caramelised colour wines)
brandy (for final fortification).

Types of Sherry: Fino, manzanilla, amontillado, oloroso, raya, palo cortado.
Name of sherry controlled. 'Sherry' comes only from Jerez. Other countries must pre-fix name immediately to that of sherry, e.g. Cream Cyprus Sherry.

Port

Area: Upper Douro, from 45 miles upstream to Spanish border.

Climate: Extreme; cold wet winters 125cm rain (50"); blisteringly hot summers (38 degrees centigrade)

Soil: Steep terraces (60 degrees slope) of schist (crystalline granite slate)

Vines: Touriga (similar to cabernet franc)
Tinta francisca (very close to pinot noir - adds colour)
Mourisca
Bastardo + others

Viticulture: Terraces blasted out of rock, each with as little as a single row of vines, trained gobelet style. Often planted on north facing slopes to avoid intense summer sun.

Vinification: Fermentation on pulp, with maximum colour extraction, achieved by constant agitation. Now usually done in autovinificator. When correct colour and sweetness is attained, wine is run off into vats containing brandy to bring alcohol up to 20% and thus arrest fermentation.

Maturation: Early in following spring wine is transported downstream to wine lodges in Vila Nova da Caia. Various styles determined by mode of maturation:

Ruby - blend of several years; matured in wood for around two years, then bottled. Ready to drink and will not improve.

Tawny - also blend of wood port, but held in wood 10 to 40 years. Commercial tawny is blend of ruby and white port.

White - a ruby type, but made with white grapes and fermented to dryness.

Vintage - the wine of an exceptional year, bottled after 2 years in wood. Needs 15 years in bottle. Decant.

Madeira

Situation: Island 36 x 15 miles, 360 miles from coast of Morocco.

Climate: Sub-tropical; 32 degrees N, warmed by Gulf Stream in winter; 27-45" rain.

Soil: Fertile volcanic tufa, enriched by ash of trees.

Vines: Sercial, Verdelho, Bual, Malvoisie.

Viticulture: Terraces with vines trained gobelet style.

Vinification: Pressed in horizontal press. Fermented to dryness for sercial and bual styles, brandy added for sweeter styles. Vinho claro.

Estufagem:	Replicates journey to E. Indies that used to be used for maturation. Estufa is a store where wines in vats or pipes are heated to 40-60 degrees centigrade for 6 months. Final fortification done after estufagem.
Styles:	Sercial - driest; taken cool as aperitif Verdelho - sweeter and softer; taken with Madeira cake. Bual - darker, fuller and sweeter; a dessert wine Malmsey - rich and luscious; malvoisie grape. Commercial blends not necessarily made from traditional grapes. High quality wines matured in solera system with date of origin. Best vintages kept as vintage wines.

Spirits

Definition: Potable spirits are beverages of high alcoholic content (usually 40% volume) obtained by distillation.

Types of still:

a) Pot still: simple boiler, connected by a head (alembic) to a condenser (worm). Batch process. Very inefficient, giving poor separation of components, giving a highly flavoured distillate.

b) Patent (Coffey) still: continuous process and very efficient, giving much more "neutral" distillate.

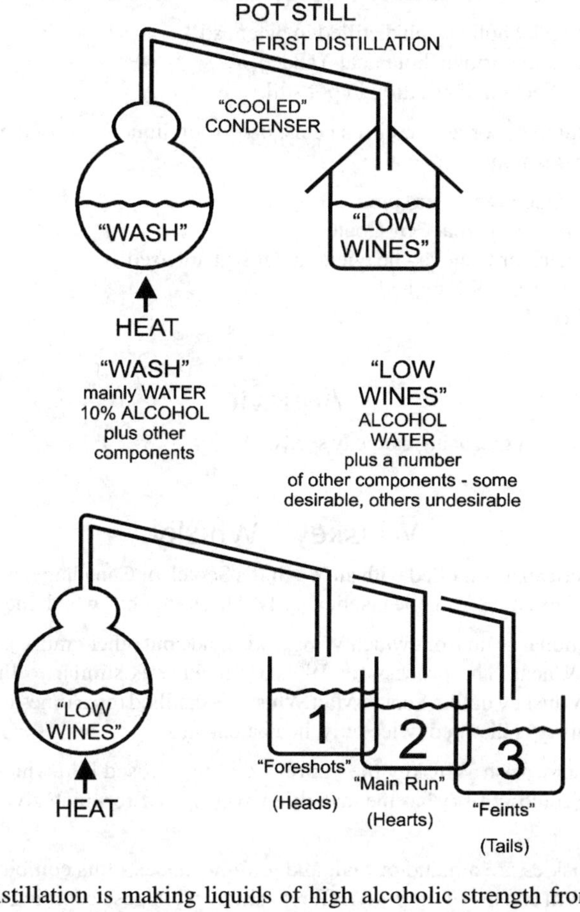

The process of distillation is making liquids of high alcoholic strength from liquids of low alcoholic strength. Because alcohol boils at a lower temperature (78°C) than water (100°C) it is possible to vapourise nearly all the alcohol from the wash. The resulting liquid is distilled again to give an even higher alcoholic content which is now known as spirit. Maturation in casks is required for the spirit to mellow and develop its full flavour.

Vodka

Pure ethanol (alcohol): the taste is alcohol. Originated in Baltic states - Poland, Latvia, Lithuania, Estonia, Russia. Produced from any starch containing crop - barley, maize, wheat, oats, rye, potatoes. Highly rectified spirit, finally passed through activated charcoal to remove all traces of flavour. Some Eastern European vodkas are flavoured.

Gin

Originated Holland 1575 - hence "Dutch courage". Juniper added to disguise coarse flavour. French for juniper is genievre, hence gin. 1736 Hogarth's "Gin Lane" and Gin Act.

Production:
1. Alcoholic wash distilled in patent still.
2. Flavourings (botanicals) added.
3. Second distillation in pot still.

Botanicals: Juniper, coriander, citrus peels, orris root, liquorice root, angelica, cinnamon, cardamoms.

Types:
London Dry - very pure
Plymouth - made by Coates
Dutch or Geneva - heavier. Patent still not used.
Old Tom - sweetened.
Cork Dry Gin

Aquavit

Scandinavian version of gin, using caraway seeds.

Whiskey - Whisky

If it's Irish or American it is spelled with an 'e' - if it's Scotch or Canadian it is spelled without an 'e'. Whiskey takes its name from the Gaelic words "Uisce Beatha" which means "water of life".

Barley is the traditional grain from which Whiskey is made but other grains are also used such as Maize, Rye and Wheat. The process for Whiskey making is similar to the process of beer production. Irish Whiskey unlike Scotch Malt Whisky is distilled three times in a pot still whereas Scotch Grain Whisky is distilled twice only, in a patent still.

During production of Irish Whiskey the malt is dried in a closed kiln which gives it a lighter flavour whereas Scotch Whisky has the malt dried over a peat fire which gives it a strong smoky flavour.

Most Scotch Whiskies are a blend of malt and grain whiskies - this combination is known as vatting. A blend will consist of up to 40 different single whiskies according to the secret recipe of each individual company.

By law Whisky for the home market must mature for a minimum of three years but in practice the minimum age is much greater. If there is an age label on a bottle it must refer to the youngest Whisky in the blend.

Bourbon Whiskey

This is the most famous of American Whiskies and by law must contain not less than 51% corn grain. It originated in Kentucky.

Rye Whiskey

This is made in Canada and USA and is made from malted barley with rye.

Malt Whisky

Those from Scotland are world famous and are made in six regions

i.e. Highlands, Lowlands, Speyside, Islands, Islay, Campbeltown.

Cognac

Area: Departements of Charente and Charents Maritime. Since phylloxera, many vineyards not replanted.

Climate: Temperate, damp, typically maritime, but with hot summers and abundant rainfall in winter.

Districts & Soils: Grande Champagne - best quality; high chalk content.
Petite Champagne - smaller proportion of chalk.
Borderies - gives cognac with greatest body.
Firm Bois, Bon Bois, Bois Ordinaires - all of lesser quality.

Vines & Wine: St Emilion (Ugni Blanc), Folle Blanche, Colombard Wine is sour, highly acid and low in alcohol (7-10%). The best cognac comes from poor quality wines. No sulphur dioxide is used.

Distillation: Twice distilled in pot still (no other type allowed).

Première chauffe (first distillation) takes 8 hours and produces milky brouillis of about 30% vol. Tete (heads), amounting to 1-1.5% of total volume, is redistilled in next 1 cre chauffe. After 3 premières chauffes, enough brouillis has been collected for the second distillation, which takes 12 hours. Tete and queue (tails) are collected separately and added to next brouillis. Bonne chauffe at 70% alcohol goes into casks of Limousin Oak for maturation, for minimum 3 years. Caramel for colouring is only additive allowed.

Styles: Grande Champagne or Grande Fine Champagne - the best cognac, with finesse and elegance.

Fine Champagne - blended from Grande & Petite, with minimum 50% Grande.

Vintage - the product of a single year; not obtainable in France due to the constant topping-up that occurs.

Old Landed - cognac shipped to UK whilst young and matured in damp London cellars. (Strictly called Early Landed, Late Bottled.)

VSOP - Very Superior Old Pale, a blend of cognacs none of which must be less than 4 years old.

*** - the basic blend of cognacs not less than 3 years old.

Armagnac

Area: Department of Gers, south of Bordeaux.

Climate: Cold windy winters, hot sunny summers. High humidity.

Districts & Soils: Bas-Armagnac - the best rich, heavy soil: clay, sand, pebbles
Tenareze - chalky slopes
Haut-Armagnac - chalky hills.

Wines: Folle Blanche, Ugni Blanc, Colombard + nine others.

Distillation: Special continuous still: alambic Armagnacais
Mandatory between 1936 and 1972. Pot still not allowed.
Strength between 58 and 63% vol.
Matured in 'chene blanc' the local Pyrenean black oak from Monlezun.
Must be completed by April 30 following vintage.

Styles: 4 appellations - Armagnac, Bas-Armagnac, Tenareze, Haut-Armagnac
Age categories similar to Cognac +
Hors d'Age - 5 years minimum, usually 10.

Rum

Definition: The distillate of products of fermented sugar-cane.

Origin: West Indies. First records Barbados 1600.

Raw materials: Molasses (residue after sugar crystallisation)
Sugar-cane juice
Concentrated sugar-cane juice
No conversion step required.

Fermentation: a) Rapid (1-2 days). Light rum.
b) Slow (up to 12 days). Dark rum.
Dunder added (residue in still after distillation).

Yeast: Cultured or natural from bagasse (pressed cane residue).

Still: a) Patent still. Light rum. 96% vol.
b) Pot still. Dark rum. 86% vol.
2 distillations.

Maturation: 3 years minimum in oak casks. Casks can be re-used because tannin and other extracts not needed. Naturally colourless; all colour is due to added caramel.

Types:

Barbados -	molasses, pot and patent, medium weight, soft, smoky, leathery
Cuban -	molasses, patent still, charcoal, very light
Demararan -	molasses, rapid fermentation, pot and patent still, dark but only medium weight.
Haitian -	cane juice, natural yeast, medium bodied, superb balance. Soil comparable with Cognac and Champagne
Jamaican -	4 types -

light: molasses, patent still
medium: cane juice and molasses, pot still
Wedderburn & Plummer: traditional, slow fermentation and dunder, pot still
high ester: as Wedderburn, but high ester content.

Vermouth

Wine-based, yet not truly wine. Name derived from German Wermut (wormwood), the plant known botanically as artemisia absinthia. Originally two main types: French (dry) and Italian (sweet). Does not now apply, as all types are produced in both countries. French industry based on Marseilles, Italian on Turin.

Base wine: Bland and insipid wines, produced in the Midi and N. Italy. French blend in some wine from Algeria. Italians use some from the plains of S. Italy (Puglia).

Herbs: Wormwood, Hyssop, Coriander, juniper, cloves, cinnamon, nutmeg, camomile, angelica, gentian, peppermint, orris root (also orange peel, quinine and other ingredients.).

Extraction: Maceration in alcohol for about 8 days, or infusion (a hot maceration, as in tea-making).

Blending: Base wine is sweetened with mistelle, the flavour extract added, artificially coloured and finally fortified with alcohol.

Finishing: Fined with tannin and gelatine.
Refrigerated at - 8 degrees centigrade for 8 days to remove unstable tartrates. Filtered. Stored for a few months to allow the flavours to 'marry'. Pasteurised and bottled.

Types: Red (rosso or rouge)

White (bianco or blanc)

Pink (rosato or rosé)

Chambery is a much lighter style, delicate and elegant. It is made in the French Alps from Alpine herbs, and has been granted the AC.

Uses: Neat, chilled or with ice. In a cocktail eg. Dry Martini - equal portions of gin and dry vermouth, a dash of orange bitters, with ice.

Liqueurs

Sweetened and flavoured spirits. Do not confuse with brandies or eaux-de-vie, which are pure unsweetened spirits, simply the products of distillation.

There are two basic methods of production:

1 Maceration or infusion, followed by filtration and sweetening eg. Grand Marnier.

2. Maceration or infusion, followed by distillation and sweetening of the distillate eg. Cointreau.

Categories (by flavour)

Herbs -

Benedictine
Drambuie
Chartreuse
Crême de Menthe
Kummel
Pernod

Fruits -

Curacao
Grand Marnier
Cherry Brandy
Southern Comfort

Beans & Kernels -

Crême de Cacao
Tia Maria
Crême de Noisette
Crême de Noyau

Beers: Ales, Stouts and Lagers

All beers are brewed. The various colours and flavours are obtained by the use of various types and colours of malt.

Malt is made by steeping barley in water for 48-72 hours until it begins to germinate. When this occurs the starches in the grain are converted to sugars. The grains are then dried by hot air in a kiln which stops any further growth.

The grain is then cooked to the required colour and flavour. Next the malt is 'cracked' in a mill producing grist. This is mixed with water at 65-66 degrees centigrade for two hours.

The flavour has now been drawn out of the malt and the liquid is run off. This liquid is now called Wort. It is now boiled with sugar syrup and hops for one and three quarter hours. The wort is strained and cooled to 15-16 degrees and allowed to ferment in a fermenting vessel. Yeast (Saccharomyces Cerevisiae) is added and fermentation continues for about seven days.

The beer now goes into a storage tank for 3-21 days (lager is longer) to await bottling or kegging, or put into casks for cask conditioned beer after 2-3 days.

The majority of beers are pasteurised and are therefore free of sediment.

The average strength of beer is approximately 4% vol. of alcohol. Some beer can be 10% sold in small bottle sizes of about 180ml (6.3 fluid ounces).

TYPES OF BEER: Bitter, Mild, Pale and Light Ale, Brown Ale, Stout, Lager.

CIDER AND PERRY: Both are alcoholic beverages of between 4% and 8% vol. Cider is made from apples and perry from pears, although each can include small quantities of other fruit. Very popular with young people.

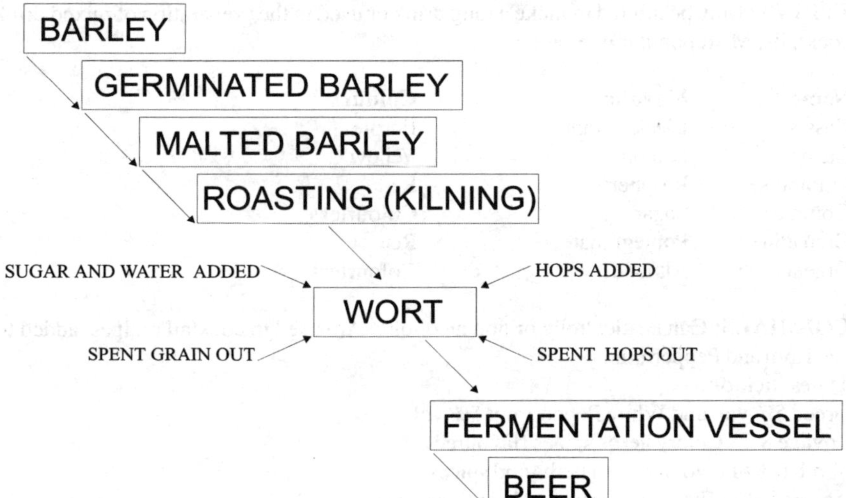

Barrelled beer is sold as real ale. The flavour of beer is deepened on the degree of roasting, the quantity of hops added, the type of yeast, initial sugar content and water quality

Natural Mineral Waters

Must originate in a ground water body or deposit and must be extracted from the ground through a spring, well or borehole. Bottled natural mineral waters may be either still or sparkling. They contain certain mineral salts beneficial to health.

All natural mineral waters must be bottled at the place of origin without any additions of sulphur and carbon dioxide.

Sparkling mineral waters are labelled, as carbonated natural mineral water, naturally carbonated neutral mineral water, or natural mineral water fortified with gas from the spring.

Name	Origin	Style	Mineral Content
Buxton	England	Still-sparkling	Low
Malvern	England	Still-sparkling	Low
Ashbourne	England	Still	Low
Highland Spring	Scotland	Still-sparkling	Low
Badoit	France	Sparkling	Low
Perrier	France	Sparkling	Low
Evian	France	Still	Low
Vichy	France	Sparkling	Medium
Spa Reine	Belgium	Still	Low
Apollinaris	Germany	Sparkling	High
San Pelligrino	Italy	Sparkling	Low
Mountain Valley	USA	Still	Low

Fruit Juices, Syrups and Cordials

FRUIT JUICES: Fresh or Bottled
SYRUPS: May be diluted to make a long drink or used in the preparation of mixed drinks and cocktails. Most popular ones are:

Name	Flavour	Colour
Cassis	Blackcurrant	Purple
Citron	Lemon	Yellow
Framboise	Raspberry	Red
Gomme	Sugar	Colourless
Grenadine	Pomegranate	Red
Orgeat	Almond	Colourless

CORDIALS: Can be alcoholic or non alcoholic. Are used in cocktail recipes, added to spirits e.g. Rum and Peppermint.
Types include:
Green 5% vol. and White Peppermint 5% vol.
Lovage 8% - Celery herbs spices flavoured
Shrub 6% - Flavoured with herbs and spices
Aniseed 5% - Flavoured from seeds of anise plant
Pink Cloves 7.5% - Made from pink cloves (Zanzibar)
Grenadine 8% - Like the syrup of the same name.

Aerated Waters and Mixers

Manufactured aerated waters contain flavourings, for example:

Lemonade, Orangeade, Cherryade, Ginger Beer and Cola.

All of these are best served chilled. They are drunk on their own or mixed with other drinks eg. Cinzano and Lemonade. Mixers are the same as manufactured aerated waters but are considered more as mixing drinks.

The most common are:

Bitter Lemon - Contains Lemons and Quinine.
Ginger Ale - Ginger flavoured, golden brown coloured.
Soda Water - Colourless
Tonic Water - Contains Quinine, colourless.
Ruschian - Peach flavoured, rose coloured.

General Questions

1. At what age, in Britain, does the law allow young persons to consume soft drinks in a licensed premises?
2. Is it an offence for under 18s to buy or drink alcohol in licensed premises or for someone to get it for them?
3. In a dining area of a licensed restaurant, can 16-18 year olds buy and consume beer, cider or perry?
4. Are children of the licensee who are under 14 years of age allowed into the bar area?
5. What is a six day licence?
6. Is it an offence to give a child under 5 years of age intoxicating liquor?
7. What is significant about 80mg of alcohol in 100mg of blood?
8. Is the passing of betting slips in a public bar permitted?
9. Is it illegal to allow prostitutes to use a public bar to obtain business?
10. Is it an offence to supply an on-duty police officer with liquor in a licensed premises?
11. Can a licensee serve any measure of wine into an unmarked glass?
12. Which wine was known as Mountain in Victorian times?
13. What word is used to describe a wine which gives impression of weight and flavour in the mouth?
14. What word is used to describe a wine which is dilute and lacking in flavour?
15. Which well known singer had a hit with a song "Little old wine drinker me"?
16. Who played the male lead role in the film "Days of Wine and Roses"?
17. What is Applejack?
18. What is a Moscow Mule?
19. What is a Bloody Mary?
20. What is a Rum Baba?
21. Name the wine used in the making of Zabaglione.
22. Which wine was known as Englishman's wine?
23. In which country are Felstar wines produced?
24. Name a grape variety with a lady's name.
25. From which country does the wine Château Musar originate?
26. Hambledon is a vineyard in which English County?
27. What is the difference between Crémant and Cramant?
28. How far should a wine glass be filled?
29. How should you store spirits and liqueurs?
30. What is the French name for a wine waiter?
31. What is a varietal wine?
32. What type of wine is Vin Jaune?
33. What is the name given to the quality Hungarian sweet wines which sell in 50cc bottles?
34. What is Bulls Blood?
35. What is Noble Rot?
36. A Greek wine flavoured with pine resin.
37. What is Pouisse-Café?
38. Name the two handed goblet for sharing a drink, usually between a bride and groom?

39. Name the substance obtained from a fish to clarify wine?
40. What is a fortified wine?
41. What is Cognac?
42. Name the tulip shaped glass used for sherry.
43. What does the word corkage indicate?
44. What is an optic?
45. Cava is a wine produced in which country?
46. What is a waiters friend?
47. What is the standard size of a wine bottle?
48. How many millilitres in a standard sized wine bottle?
49. What does 40% proof on a bottle of spirits indicate?
50. Which wine growing district uses a black cockerel as their symbol?
51. What colour shows at the side of a glass in very young white wine?
52. What colour shows on the sides of a glass of very young red wine?
53. In which country was the phylloxera louse first identified?
54. Name the Greek god of wine.
55. Does the island of Hawaii produce wine?
56. What does the word "astringent" indicate?
57. Pourriture, Edelfaule and Botrytis Cinera: are they all affected by noble rot?
58. How was the Phylloxera disease overcome?
59. Where is the Valley of Plenty?
60. Where is the Bay of Plenty?
61. Where is the Valley of the Moon?
62. What is a hybrid wine?
63. Name two wineries from the Napa Valley.
64. Name two wineries from the Sonoma County?
65. Name four US states that produce wine excluding California and New York.
66. Ouzo is a drink flavoured with ....?
67. Pastis is a drink flavoured with ....?
68. What is an autovinificator?
69. Where did gin originate?
70. Vodka is produced from ....?
71. Name three malt whisky distilleries in the Grampian Highlands.
72. In which country will you find the Lamberhurst vineyard?
73. Which drink did Noah say tasted of sinners?
74. Name the largest wine growing region of Switzerland.
75. Which country can claim that most of its wines are directly descended from the pre-phylloxera European varieties?
76. What is Pisco?
77. What is the classic wine from the region of Valais in Switzerland?
78. Where is the liqueur Rosa produced?
79. What do the words Minosegi Bor on the label of a bottle of Hungarian wine indicate?
80. Burgenland is a wine region of which country?

81. What is the Bouquet of a wine?
82. What is meant by a dry wine?
83. What does the term sur lie indicate?
84. A rough fiery brandy produced from the residue left after pressed grape skins, pips and stalks is known as?
85. Mise en Boutelles on a wine label indicates....?
86. A wooden cask holding 225 is called a ....?
87. How many glasses are obtained from a standard 75cl bottle of wine?
88. How many glasses are obtained from a standard bottle of fortified wine?
89. Name four facts which by law must appear on a wine label.
90. Ernest and Julio Gallo winery is in which region of California?
91. Champagne is the king of wines and ....?
92. What is a gill?
93. What is meant by the term 6 out?
94. Monitoring the amount of alcohol you drink can be measured in terms of ....?
95. Name two of the principal vineyards of New Zealand?
96. Name three wine regions of Australia?
97. Warmed cups are used in the service of which drink?
98. Which substance in some red wines gives lasting power and adds flavour and body?
99. Must is a wine term for ....?
100. By British law how long should Scotch Whisky be in cask before selling?
101. Is bastardo a grape variety, a cask or a type of wine glass?
102 What name is given to the process of which yeast breaks down grape sugar into alcohol.
103. Why are bottles of wine stored on their sides?
104. Are publicans and hoteliers breaking the law by not displaying tariffs for coin operated phones on their premises?
105. What is "grog"?
106. What medical handicap did Dom Perignon suffer from?
107. How many litres in a hectolitre?
108 Aloha Coffee Liqueur is produced in which country?
109. Amaretto liqueur is flavoured with apricot kernals. True or False?
110. The wine area in the region of Lake Balaton is in which country?
111. Cornas is a wine producing district in which wine region?
112. Fontanella is a sparkling wine from which country?
113. Château Grillet is a wine producing area of which region?
114. What measurement of liquid also gives its name to a gun?
115. Tiger milk is a white wine from which country?
116. Fiasco is the name used to describe the .... of some Chianti red wine.
117. What name is given to the inverted bottom of a champagne bottle?
118. What is the English translation of the Italian wine Est Est Est?
119. Thomas Jefferson, third president of the USA was very fond of which brand of Champagne?
120 What product is made from distilled wine?
121. What is a vintage port?

122. How many vintage ports are declared each decade?
123. What is the Gobelet system used for?
124. The Singleton, Longman and Mar Lodge are all ....?
125. The South American country which produces most wine is ....?
126. When sampling wine the order of assessment is ....?
127. In 1832 an Irishman invented the continuous still, was his name (a) Patrick Coffey (b) Michael Coffey (c) Aeneas Coffey?
128. The wines from Northern Burgundy are made principally from which grape variety?
129. Chablis is produced from which grape variety?
130. It is common practice to serve coffee beans floating in which drink?
131. The major alcohol of wine is ....?
132. The base spirit of Grand Marnier is ....?
133. Name the winery owned by the American comedians the Smothers Brothers.
134. For what reason should you decant wine?
135. Who patented the first corkscrew?
136. What do the letters M.W. stand for in the world of wine?
137. Bourgueil is a wine district of which region?
138. Red wines should be served at what temperature?
139. White wines should be served at what temperature?
140. Sparkling wine should be served at what temperature?
141. What is Dutch Courage?
142. What is the Scandinavian version of gin using caraway seeds?
143. Which area of Australia produces the largest percentage of wine?
144. In which area of Australia were vines first planted?
145. Which islands produce malt whisky?
146. What is whiskey sour?
147. Name the popular liqueur invented in New Orleans in 1860.
148. Mateus Rosé comes from which Portuguese region?
149. Name two wines from Bordeaux.
150. Name one red and one white wine from Burgundy.
151. Name two white wines from Alsace.
152. Name one red and one rose wine from Provence.
153. Name one red, one white and one sparkling wine from the Rhône.
154. Name one red, one white and one sparkling wine from Loire.
155. Name two wines from Piedmont.
156. Name two wines from Umbria.
157. Name two wines from Tuscany.
158. Name two wines from Marches.
159. Name two wines from Campania.
160. Name two wines from Veneto.
161. Sekt is a sparkling wine from which country?
162. Perry is a drink made from ....?
163. The letters D.O.M. are associated with which drink?

164. At what temperature does alcohol vaporise?
165. What wine is used in the dish Tripe a la Caen?
166. Wine growing areas around the earth lie between the latitudes 20-40 degrees North and South of the equator. True or False?
167. Where did Christ perform the miracle of turning water into wine?
168. What is average ph range for wine.
169. How is the alcoholic content of drinks measured?
170. What is a unit of alcohol?
171. How many grams of alcohol in one unit?
172. On average, how long does it take the body to lose one unit of alcohol?
173. What is a sensible and safe upper limit of units for a man and a woman to drink per week?
174. Who are mostly at risk at these levels and well below these levels?
175. What was the Methuen Treaty?
176. What wines are put in a Bocksbeutel?
177. Santa Marta wine comes from which country?
178. Santa Rita wine comes from which country?
179. In which country are the world's heaviest drinkers?
180. In which country are the world's second heaviest drinkers?
181. What position is the UK in the league of heaviest drinkers?
182. What is the base ingredient of Sake?
183. What is the base ingredient of Midori?
184. What is the base ingredient of Baileys Irish Cream?
185. What is the base ingredient of Slowboat?
186. Old Nick is a white rum produced in which area?
187. In which wine region is Graves situated?
188. Angustura Bitter is produced in which country?
189. How did it get its name?
190. What is Byrrh?
191. What is Cap Corse?
192. What is Lillet?
193. Picolit is a wine from which region?
194. What type of drink is Baies do Houx?
195. What type of drink is Sureau?
196. What type of drink is Prunelle?
197. Where is Clos de Val Vineyard?
198. Where is Clos du Pape Vineyard?
199. Where is Clos Avocat Vineyard?
200. Provence was the home of a world famous painter, who was he?
201. Which of the following countries produce most wine, Russia or West Germany?
202. Which of the following countries produce most wine, Romania or Portugal?
203. Which of the following countries produce most wine, Chile or Greece?
204. Almaden is a brandy from which country?
205. What type of drink is Château Tanunda?

206. What does a slimmer's breakfast cocktail consist of?
207. At what temperature does ethyl alcohol freeze?
208. Which wine was known as elevenses in Victorian times?
209. Marko is a red wine from which country?
210. Name the ingredients in a "dog nose" cocktail.
211. Name the ingredients in a "bucks head" cocktail.
212. Which is the largest selling spirit in the world?
213. What is a Jigger?
214. What is Blue Burgundy?
215. Where is the liqueur Lakka made?
216. Matured Cognacs are removed from oak casks and are placed in carboys. What is a carboy?
217. Metoxa is a brandy produced in which country?
218. What is a Fine Champagne?
219. Madeira is the Portuguese word for ....?
220. Stock 84 is a brandy produced in which country?
221. Name the smallest AOC vineyard in France.
222. How many litres in a case of wine?
223. Spring Moon is a wine produced in which country?
224. Name the region which produces the white wine Fiano.
225. Which spirit is made from dates.
226. What is the alcoholic strength of still wines?
227. What is the alcoholic strength of fortified wines?
228. Which vineyard uses a stork on its bottle label for its white wine?
229. What body was set up to promote Australian wines in UK in 1986?
230. Taste buds are concentrated on different parts of the tongue. Where are the following situated?
    (a) Sweetness
    (b) Saltiness
    (c) Acidity
    (d) Bitterness
231. What is Australia's share of the UK wine market?
232. In which area is the French Colombard grape variety most widely planted?
233. Where was the wine Lachryma Montis (Tears of the Mountain) produced?
234. Film producer Francis Ford Cappola owns a vineyard in which wine region of California?
235. Which firm is the world's largest winemaker?
236. Name the wine produced at Villeneuve-Loubet, the birthplace of the world famous chef Escoffier.
237. In which year was the first vintage port produced?
238. What is the relationship between Lamborghini and Lago di Trasimeno Umbria?
239. O'Higgins is a wine producing region of which country?
240. What is a Mickey Finn?
241. Where is the largest pot still in the world situated?
242. What is its capacity in litres and in gallons?

243. What happens to sauterne wine if it fails to reach 13% alcohol content?
244. In what capacity is ox blood used in wine making?
245. How did Rioja take its name?
246. When fining red wines what is the average quantity of egg whites used?
247. What name is given to the absorbent clay used for fining?
248. Name the person who founded the Hospice de Beaune?
249. From which region does Haut Brion originate?
250. In which wine growing area is Toul?
251. The description 'basket press' on a label indicates ....?
252. Where is wine glass bay?
253. How does red wine protect against heart disease?
254. Which ancient city centre layout is shaped like a champagne cork?
255. Who or what is Robbie Dubh?
256. Which Duke was drowned in a butt of Malmsey?
257. Which island was known as the island of trees?
258. Which islands are known as the Islands of the Blessed?
259. Which grape variety is known as the King of Alsace?
260. Which is the only red grape variety granted A.O.C. status in Alsace?
261. Which country has the greatest number of vineyards, Australia, South Africa or New Zealand?
262. Name five male film stars who were cast as drunks in a film.
263. Name the films in the above (question 262).
264. Name five female film stars who were cast as drunks in a film.
265. Name the films in question 264.
266. What was Queen Victoria's favourite drink?
267. Shortly before meeting his doom, Don Giovanni sings the praises of which Italian wine?
268. Which village in Côte d'Or has a claim to fame other than that of its wine?
269. What name links a peach nectar, a Sicilian composer, a Venetian painter and a refreshing combination of sparkling wine?
270. Caipirinha is the national drink of which country?
271. Which country has the highest level of deaths from alcoholic poisoning in the world?
272. California's first Sauvignon Blanc grapes were planted in 1878. From which famous Bordeaux Estate did they come from?
273. What is unusual about the labels on bottles of the top wines from Kenwood Vineyards?
274. Which Egyptian King on his death bed had a large quantity of wine to accompany his spirit on its journey to the after life?
275. How did the Christine Woods vineyard get its name?
276. What was the favourite grape variety of bootleggers during prohibition in the USA?
277. Name the first woman to set up a winery in the NAPA valley.
278. Where were the oldest grape seeds in the world discovered?
279. What was the ancient capital of Champagne?
280. Inky-Pinky was used to describe: (a) an instrument (b) a type of wine (c) small beer.
281. What alcoholic drinks are junior ratings on board British warships allowed?
282. Name the smallest distillery in Scotland.

283. One of the stongest beers in the world Samichlaus (14% ABV) is brewed only once a year on December 6th especially for the Christmas Season. Where is it made?
284. Where was Reindeer beer made?
285. The Gaelic name for this drink is "the drink that satisfies" name the drink.
286. Name the drink created in the 16th century on the shores of Lake Como as a reward to a painter by the beautiful inn-keeper's daughter whose face he used as a model in one of his paintings.
287. Name the grape variety used as a wild bird deterrent.
288. Which English wine has been nicknamed Electric Soup and Cheeky Water?
289. What was George Orwell's favourite pub called?
290. In Shakespeare's Henry IV Falstaff was accused of selling his soul for which drink?
291. These two singers sang a saucy song about Madeira ....
292. Who banished the gamay grape variety in the northern area of Burgundy because he felt it did not suit the area?
293. What are coolers?
294. What do the letters C A M R A stand for?
295. When was the prohibition period in the USA?
296. Which grape variety is so called because the grapes form a long way from the flowers?
297. Back in 1925 a Professor Abraham Perold experimented by breeding a cross between the classic Pinot Noir grape and the Hermitage and produced which grape variety?
298. Which whiskey was named after a racehorse?
299. Where is Tyrconnell whiskey produced?
300. In Chablis the chardonnay grape variety is also known as ....?
301. In Austria the most popular red grape variety is called ....?
302. According to legend which King was baptised with drops of Armagnac?
303. In which museum will you see a 19th century wine press weighing 18 tons which relied on two whole oak trees, one to support the trays of grapes, the other to be lowered down to crush the fruit?
304. A vintage Armagnac should specify two dates, what are they?
305. How many litres of wines distils a single litre of Armagnac?
306. Raki or "lions milk" as its known locally is the favourite drink of which country?
307. When does harvesting of grapes take place south of the Equator?
308. Château Rayas is the only wine that has a 100% of this grape variety ....
309. What do the three roasted coffee beans served in a flamed glass of Sambuca indicate?
310. In which wine regions would you find Mount Helen and Mount Helena?
311. Where does the drink Alexanders originate?
312. Which prime grape variety is called Blue Pyrenees in the Victorian Pyrenees?
313. Château Petrus is made with 100% of which grape variety?
314. Is Gin Gin a drink, a type of container or the name of a place?
315. Are wines made in Denmark?
316. Shiraz is grown in Tasmania, true or false?
317. Which Scottish distillery matures its entire whisky production only in sherry casks?
318. The Australians have developed a method which will separate the different elements present in wine. What is it called?

319. What is the French Code Napoleon which is prominent in the Burgundy region?
320. What did Robert Louis Stevenson buy for 65 francs and a glass of brandy on one of his travels in France?
321. King James I issued a proclamation forbidding the use of timber in the manufacture of what end product?
322. Which is France's oldest brandy?
323. Tarrawingee is a red Australian wine so called after an ancient Aboriginal word for which bird?
324. Domaine de St Julian is not a great claret but it achieved fame in Cirencester, a Gloucestershire town, why?
325. What is the connection between these three malt whisky distilleries, Tamnayuun, Grampian and Bruichladdich?
326. Where are the Prince Albert vineyards?
327. Anne Riesling was a wine produced in Australia up to the late 1980s. What is the name of her sister wine still in production?
328. This village near Macon in Burgundy is named after a famous grape variety.
329. Which drink is known as "Treasure of the Rhine"?
330. This grape variety is known as Cencibel in La Mancha and as .... in Rioja.
331. What is Margaret Thatcher's favourite alcoholic drink?
332. Royalty helped to make this wine fashionable - it was apparently drunk at the wedding of Queen Victoria and Prince Albert?
333. Is Guinness regularly imported into Ireland?
334. What type of drink is Crested Red?
335. Where is the drink Three Stills produced?
336. In which Burgundy village were the first ever photographs taken?
337. The famed Italian vinegar Balsamic is produced from which grape variety?
338. In which two wine districts is the soil predominantly chalk?
339. Southern Comfort is made in which state?
340. The French wine-making region which is closest to the German border is .....?
341. The main flavouring ingredient in London Gin is ....?
342. The mulled wine "The Bishop" is made with which ingredients?
343. The mulled wine "The Cardinal" is made with which ingredients?
344. What are the ingredients for the cocktail "Corpse Reviver"?
345. What are the ingredients for the cocktail "Everybodys Irish"?
346. What are the ingredients for the cocktail "Bosom Caresser"?
347. What are the ingredients for the cocktail "Earthquake"?
348. What is the difference between a Whisky Punch and a Hot Toddy?
349. Which French town is named after the god Bolonus?
350. The words Deo Optimo Maximo associated with champagne are inscribed over the main door of which Cathedral?
351. Which famous English actress bought a vineyard in California in the 1800's?
352. Which type of drink is a Galway Pipe?
353. What is the record price paid for a corkscrew?
354. What kind of wine is "Cold Duck"?

355. The largest malt whisky distillery is not in Scotland. In which country is it situated?
356. In which country is the World's oldest brewery situated?
357. What are the names of the two non-alcoholic drinks sold by Prince Charles' firm Duchy Originals?
358. The first alcoholic lemonade was produced in Australia. What was it called?
359. What was unusual about the wine labels on wine bottles from the Garonne on Tarn regions of SW France and supplied to various supermarkets and restaurants in 1995?
360. What are the contents of the non-alcoholic cocktail "Above all"?
361. Which Spanish wine has been dubbed el vino de la alegria (the wine of joy)?
362. Tsar Alexander II of Russia had his bottles of Prestige champagne made of crystal as his previous bottles looked like any other. This champagne house has carried on producing them ever since. Name the champagne house.
363. Grenadine is made from which fruit?
364. Which champagne house has its bottles decorated with a reproduction of the Legion d'Honneur ribbon?
365. Parra is a raw spirit made from the lees of wine making. Where is it made?
366. In the drinks industry what do A.S.D. stand for?
367. What is France's most southerly A.O.C.?
368. Which French village is derived from the Latin meaning "Merry City"?
369. The words "Sans Alcool" are prominently displayed on the labels of some French drinks. What do they indicate?
370. What does the word "clos" indicate?
371. Which was the first wine taken to outer space?
372. After trebbiano which is Italy's mostly used white grape variety?
373. A giant bottle of claret produced to celebrate the allied victory in the Second World War was sold in 1995 for:
(a) £2,500 (b) £16,363 (c) £36,277?
374. The label on the above bottle showed which sign?
375. How many of the giant claret bottles by Château Mouton - Rothschild in 1945 were produced (a) 100 (b) 24 (c) 1945?
376. Which drink is known as "poor man's port"?
377. The Lamberhurst vineyard in Kent was sold in 1995 by which construction magnate?
378. What price did he obtain for his vineyard and stock?
379. A case of Romanee-Conti 1978 (12 bottles) sold in 1995 fetched a record price at Christies in London. Was it (a) £200,000 (b) £23,100 (c) £46,200?
380. How much per glass (6) for the above wine?
381. Jean Martell who founded the Martell Company came from which island?
382. Which former head of a famous Cognac Company died in June 1995?
383. How did the drink "Porter" get its name?
384. What type of drink is a "Bishop's Finger"?
385. Which Dutch beer has its name, crest and colours to symbolise the Dutch Royal Family tree?
386. Which beer forms ice crystals at -4 degrees centigrade which are then removed in the brewing process to make a smooth yet strong beer?

387. This beer is traditionally drunk with a slice of lime in the bottle neck.
388. This beer is named after the mythical creature part deer and part dragon that fathered Confucius and is therefore viewed as a symbol of good fortune.
389. In which Irish city is Murphy's stout produced?
390. Which city is famous for a beer named after it and for producing Skoda cars?
391. What drink immortalised by Shakespeare was produced for children and nursing mothers?
392. What was the favourite tipple of George Washington, first President of the United States?
393. What is distinctive about the beer Schlenker-La Rauchbier?
394. Which country has a famous beer called Singa?
395. Dragon Eye is (a) a Chinese wine (b) a Chinese grape variety (c) a Chinese beer?
396. Buzbag is (a) a Turkish red wine (b) a Turkish grape variety (c) a Turkish wine container?
397. The red Turkish wine Naema is named after which animal slain by hercules?
398. What does the term Rancio indicate when appertaining to brandy?
399. Which hybrid variety of grape is banned throughout the EC on quality grounds?
400. Bruno Paillard the champagne house puts which date on every bottle of their champagne?
401. What ban on spirits was lifted in June 1995?
402. Who invented Babycham?
403. When does a member of the Krug family first taste champagne?
404. Which city imports ethanol produced from surplus cheap red wine to fuel its fleet of alcohol-fuelled buses?
405. Which country introduced new restrictions in 1995 on its drink driving laws by reducing the blood alcohol content from .7 grams of alcohol to .5 grams per litre of blood?
406. What are ingredients of Pousse Rapiere (Sword Thrust)?
407. Where was Europe's most northerly commercial vineyard situated?
408. How many separate bars are there in the Palace of Westminster if we include cafeterias and tearooms which are licensed?
409. Which champagne house backs the Admirals Cup at Cowes?
410. Which champagne house backs the English National Opera and the English Cricket Team?
411. Which champagne house backs several Grand Prix races?
412. One bottle of wine can equal how many units?
413. Which vodka is named after a racehorse?
414. What are the ingredients for the cocktail Virgin Mary (a Hangover cure!)?
415. What are the ingredients for the cocktail Virgin Bull Shot?
416. The letters R.D. after a champagne ie. Bollinger R.D. signifies what?
417. What is the translation of the pink champagne Oeil de Perdrix?
418. In 1995 British Airways went to great lengths to find a champagne that held its bubbles in flight. Which champagne was selected?
419. Alcohol is twice as potent in flight than at sea level. True or False?
420. British scientists have developed a machine which can be used in the wine industry to identify which substances are in it. What are they?
421. Where is Taybeh Golden Beer produced?
422. Crianza refers to the amount of time the wine has to spend in oak and bottles before it can be sold. True or False?
423. Tinto de Toro is the local name for which grape variety?

424. King John of Magna Carta fame was crowned in which French town?
425. What is the major component of grape juice?
426. Why is Pinot Meuniere called "Millers vine"?
427. Muffa is a term used to describe?
428. This word is used to describe the crop diminishing phenomenon caused by strong winds and cold wet weather.
429. What ingredients are in the cocktail Bellini?
430. In 1996 a Japanese tourist paid £10,000 for a single bottle of drink at Heathrow's duty free shop. What was the drink?
431. Where is the most expensive place in the World to buy a bottle of beer?
432. Of all the vines grown in Cognac 95% are of this variety.
433. Indian brewers make a sparkling wine from which fruit (not grapes)?
434. Name Germany's oldest wine village.
435. Which drink is sold in a lightbulb shaped bottle and has an alcoholic content of 8.4%?
436. Hugh Williams nose is as famous as showbiz hooters belonging to the likes of Barbra Streisand and Barry Manilow. What is his occupation?
437. The exact blend of about a dozen ingredients that go into the manufacture of Gordons Gin is a secret held by how many people?
438. The world record for the biggest Irish Coffee is?
439. Why are German lesbians making their own wine?
440. Malvacea is the local dessert wine from which island?
441. What is the alcohol strength of Communion wine?
442. A pill called Acamprosat is used by drinkers for what purpose?
443. Which well known British singer bought a vineyard and plans to produce his own wine?
444. The Scots and Irish joined forces to defend which drink?
445. Which drink is produced from the fruit of the elephant tree?
446. Casablanca is a wine region of which country?
447. Samuel Becket's favourite whiskey was?
448. Which Frenchman gave 60 million gold francs to help re-establish vineyards in Israel in 1882?
449. Which drink is produced at Lady's Well Brewery?
450. The Royal College of Physicians criticised which football club for promoting its own brand of whisky?
451. Which drink had its label changed after criticism that it was too appealing to young people?
452. Which is the only château in Bordeaux making its own wooden casks?
453. The popping of champagne corks could soon become out of date. Why is this?
454. What is a hard up distillery in Russia paying off its £450,000 tax debts in?
455. Which champagne house launched their latest vintage La Grande Dame Rosé on the market in 1996 at £110 a bottle?
456. In the James Bond film 'Golden Eye' which champagne was kept in the glove compartment of his car?
457. How many distinct types of Tequila are there?
458. Which Bollinger champagne was served at the Prince of Wales' stag party at Whites?
459. Bollinger 1985 Rosé was served at which famous cricketer's wedding in 1994?

460. What is the name of the trophy for the top English wine award?
461. What is the duty on a bottle of wine in France?
462. What is the duty on a bottle of spirits in the UK?
463. Wine merchant Thomas Bignould created which major insurance company in 1797?
464. Which famous author once said that the town of Jerez ought to be in heaven?
465. Cutty Sark whisky insured themselves against paying out £1 million on what event?
466. What grape variety is used to make red wine in Beaujolais?
467. In South Africa who or what is known as the "Cape Doctor"?
468. Which was the first major wine region in the world to be demarcated in 1756?
469. Which New Zealand wine region produces the world's eastern-most grapes?
470. This wine region is near the international date line and was named Poverty Bay by Captain Cook in 1769?
471. What is the connection of the famous "Don" and work by a Scottish artist and Sandeman?
472. Which region is known as the Chardonnay capital of New Zealand?
473. How old must Bourbon whiskey be before it can be legally sold?
474. What is the predominating grain used in bourbon?
475. A special beer has been brewed for the 1996 Norwich and Norfolk beer festival to commemorate a royal event?
476. How did the drink Campari get its name?
477. What is the record for the longest flight of a cork from an untreated and unheated champagne 4ft (1.22m) bottle from level ground?
478. What is Norfolk Oyster?
479. What is Norfolk Smuggler?
480. To celebrate Norwich Cathedral's 900th Anniversary Bishops Barrel was made for the Bishop of Norwich. What was it?
481. Saint Bernadette of Lourdes is buried in which Burgundy town?
482. Why are scientists baffled about the bubbles in Guinness?
483. In which year was prohibition introduced in the USA?
484. Arthur Bell has introduced a new malt whisky in honour of which event?
485. Which politician has two Yorkshire terriers called Whisky and Soda?
486. Name the drink which Victor Hugo called "the liquor of the Gods".
487. What do the locals call "Shetland Roses"?
488. Francisco Morales who died in 1997 invented which famous cocktail?
489. Who bought a collection of Château d'Yquem wines which contained a bottle for each year from 1855 to 1990 for $1 million.
490. Which drink has a two bottle in one design which when poured both liquids merge through a single opening to form this drink?
491. Which well known wine is the centre of a feud that has split one of Frances best known families because of a takeover bid?
492. What marketing stunt did an Italian wine merchant use to promote the sales of his wines?
493. Which of the following contain most congeners and therefore produce the worst hangover (a) Brandy (b) Gin (c) Vodka?
494. Myrrh, a gift from the three wise men to the infant Jesus, can be found in which drink?
495. What is the name of the drinks industry body set up to promote responsible drinking?

What do you know about drink?

496. What type of drink is cats pee on a Gooseberry Bush?
497. Which champagne house has a soundless train controlled by laser beams which takes you through 11 miles of cellars?
498. All the Kings of France were crowned from 1180 to 1825 in which French town?
499. Which alcoholic drink was banned in Europe and America earlier this century because it was driving people insane?
500. Van Gogh hacked off his ear while under the influence of which alcoholic drink?
501. What is the alcoholic strength of Absinthe.
502. Where is Château Lizard produced?
503. La Mare vineyard is situated on which island?
504. Why are traditional bistros called Bouchons in Lyon?
505. An Irishman has come up with a technique which will keep the head on beer and lager for over two hours. What is it?
506. Englishman Guy Williams broke which French drink record in 1990?
507. Which drink is to replace grain spirits at ministerial banquets in China?
508. Which baby made a comeback after being discarded for several years because it was not trendy enough?
509. Biska is a Croation spirit made from which popular Christmas plant?
510. Black Death is a brand name for which type of drink?
511. How much did Andrew Lloyd Webber's wine collection fetch in May 1997?
512. How much did an American corkscrew patented by A.T. Russell in 1862 fetch at Christies in London in 1997?
513. Which malt whisky was first distilled on Christmas Day 1887?
514. What type of drink is Shochu?
515. Which is the oldest distillery in Scotland?
516. Who or what is Towser?
517. Which whisky is named after the Valley of the Deer?
518. Which grape variety grown in Ontario is named after a famous French first world war general?
519. What recent additional information is on the labels of Mondavis wines of California?
520. What type of ritual is Ikki Nomi?
521. What type of drink is Pigs Nose?
522. Which Scottish distillery holds a Guinness Book of Records achievement for its cat?
523. Which is the only Highland Malt Whisky to be distilled, matured and bottled at its own distillery?
524. The Maltese Cross has been used by which Champagne house as its house crest since 1798?
525. Jewish tradition decrees that during PASSOVER how many glasses of wine must be drunk to celebrate the exodus of Jews out of Egypt?
526. What is the difference between Kosher and non Kosher wine?
527. Which British football club has its origins in a whiskey distillery?
528. What type of drink is a Blackstone?
529. What is a FOB?
530. What is Red Brandy?
531. Name one thing we can both eat and drink

532. Suppose a dad leaves two 16 year old sons outside in a pub garden while he goes inside to get three pints of beer. Two of the drinks are going to under 18 year olds who are not going to be eating at the pub. Is the dad breaking the law or is the licensee who served the drinks committing an offence?
533. Guinness has introduced which system to provide lager and stout drinkers with the best pint ever dispensed?
534. A lager head means publicans will have to fill less liquid into glasses which means they can expect to get how many extra pints out of a barrel?
535. Which Andrew was to blame for destroying the $3 million contents of a wine cellar in a Miami restaurant?
536. What is the connection between a champagne bottle and Ireland?
537. In which French wine region is Morvan (Celtic for Black Mountain)?
538. The name of the cat that replaced Towser at Glenfiddich distillery is:
A. Misty B. Bonnie C. Amber ?
539. A 19th century English corkscrew patented by Thomason fetched how much in 1997 at Christies in London?
540. Which vineyard has its labels inscribed with the image of a small boy who has just had his bottom smacked?
541. Which country bans labels on wines with any link between sex nudity and alcohol?
542. “Who Cares” is a wine from which country?
543. How did the vineyard Montre-Cul (“Show Arse”) get its name?
544. Which American movie actor has launched Pale Rider ale which is named after his 1958 Western?
545. The earliest Bordeaux wine harvest on record began on what date?
546. What was unusual about the surroundings where King Alfonso XIII had lunch when he visited the Torres Bodega in Villa Franca in 1904.
547. Which is the most northerly malt whisky distillery in Scotland?
548. Name the six classic malt whisky range?
549. What is QUAICH used for?
550. In which Irish town is there a new wine museum?
551. What was the name of the two handled mug from which drink is shared which featured in Thomas Hardy’s “Far from the Madding Crowd”?
552. The makers of Laphroaig a malt whisky from Islay recently lost a legal battle concerning their whisky. What was it?
553. Which English Queen had the nickname "Brandy Nan".
554. What is the world's biggest spirit brand?
555. What is the world's best selling whisky?
556. Which UK brand of spirits is the best performer and comes ninth in the world's top selling spirits?
557. A survey compiled by three French economists concluded that what determins the price of a bottle of wine is?
558. Muscatel Commando is a very popular Californian wine with which group of people?
559. Josef Jacobs a wine expert achieved which distinction prior to his 100th birthday?
560. What are the ingredients of the Irish drink called Craic?

561. Which spirit made from Scotch Whisky and tastes like a good whisky cannot be called by that name?
562. What is the Italian equivalent to the French Vin de Pays and German Landwein?
563. Prosecco the dry to lightly sweet white wine usually bubbly, comes from which Italian area?
564. Which drink is named after Aunt Mary?
565. Where would you find an underground winery with year round drip irrigation?
566. Which Australian wine region is noted for its red limestone?
567. What does the French term "Terroir" indicate?
568. What aspect should a vineyard in the southern hemisphere have?
569. Which famous ex footballer has his name and picture on some Italian wines?
570. Mannochmore Distillery achieved what distinction with its first ever malt whisky?
571. An Irish liqueur has been produced to commemorate the 150 years of the great famine. Is it named (A) Celtic Spirit, (B) Celtic Pride or (C) Celtic Crossing?
572. What are low wines?
573 The French name for coffee with brandy or rum and flamed is?
574 What medical condition did Jack Daniels die of?
575 Which fungus was called God is Good by the English?
576 This American jazzman died of alcoholic poisoning in 1943.
577 This plant belonging to the cannabis family is used in which popular drink?
578 According to legend an Aztec Princess called Xolhiti is associated with what type of drink?
579 What nationality was John Jameson?
580 Which American President built his own whiskey distillery?
581 Two hundred and fifty years of recent British history is immortalized on beer bottles in a museum set up at which British brewery?
582 How many pubs are there in London's Oxford Street?
583 Meg Ryan, Placido Domingo, Racquel Welch, Sharon Stone, Paul Newman, Kim Bassinger were used to advertise which drink?
584 Bagpiper whisky is the product of which country?
585 According to French scientists a few drinks a day makes women more .....?
586 When was the first official breath test for car drivers introduced?
587 Where is Red Cock whisky produced?
588 What new record did Chef Keith Parkyn set in December 1997?
589 Under French Law any six year old Cognac or five year old Armagnac can legitimately call itself what?
590 Which grape variety dominates the wine production of Switzerland?
591 How did hotel maid Helen Lena pull the plug on a couples celebrations?
592 Which Highland Malt whisky was the favourite of Scottish poet Robert Burns?
593 For which purpose can alginate beads be used in the making of wine?
594 The town of Champagn is situated in which country?
595 For which purpose is the drug campral used in the drinks industry?
596 Which well known Bordeaux town has a church with a restaurant on its roof?
597 A 1998 research report on spending in Europe put which country top for spending on alcoholic drinks?

598 The term vintage indicates?
599 What is the meaning of assemblage?
600 Three sheets to the wind is a slang synonym for?

FRANCE

1. The initials A.O.C. indicate ....
2. The initials V.D.Q.S. indicate ....
3. What is vin de pays?
4. What is vin de table?
5. Newly harvested wine intended to be consumed within months is called ....
6. What does mise en bouteilles indicate?
7. Negociant is the name given to ....
8. What does the term Sur Lie indicate?
9. Blanc de Noir indicates ....
10. What is a Barrique?
11. The term ullage indicates ....
12. What is the frenchman Charmat famous for?
13. What type of wine is Vin Jaune?
14. What is Hospices de Beaune famous for?
15. Who was the widow Clicquot?
16. In which wine region is Edelzwicker produced?
17. Who was Eleanor of Aquitaine?
18. The tiny chapel of St. Christopher tops which hillside vineyard?
19. Name the wine region which is situated between Nice and Perignon.
20. In which region is the Ardeche?
21. The A.O.C. Côte du Rhône was granted in which decade of the 20th Century?
22. How many departments are there in Côtes du Rhône?
23. Name the famous rosé wine of the Rhône region.
24. Beaujolais region covers a 45 miles long stretch of mainly granite hills south of Mâcon in southern Burgundy. Which region lies south of this area?
25. Wines labelled Beaujolais come from south of the region, true or false?
26. Beaujolais Villages comes from about 40 villages north of the region, true or false?
27. The release date for Beaujolais Nouveau is ....
28. When did Côtes de Buzet achieve A.O.C. status?
29. In which area of France is Buzet?
30. Name two red wines from the Loire.
31. What is the longest river in France?
32. Which French city was the site of the ancient Palace of the Popes?
33. Who was the first Pope to reside in this French city?
34. In which district are the "roasted vineyards" situated?
35. Who is the patron saint of French winemakers?
36. What is "remuage"?

37. The British refer to Bourdeaux wine as ....
38. The wine Pouilly Fumé is produced in which French region?
39. The wine Pouilly Fuissé is produced in which French region?
40. The grape variety Pinot de la Loire is also know as ....?
41. Côtes de Nuits and Côtes de Beaune is also known as Côtes ....?
42. Which part of the Bordeaux areas produces the world's finest wines?
43. In legend which two wine areas are named after the two daughters of a medieval lord?
44. What is the Mistral?
45. What is Petite Champagne?
46. In which wine region will you find Fin Bois, Bons Bois, Bois Ordinaires?
47. What do the letters V.S.O.P. stand for?
48. Where is Armagnac produced?
49. What is known as the angels share?
50. What is responsible for the blackened roofs and walls in the town of Cognac?
51. How long should a bottle of 3 star brandy be aged for?
52. How long should a bottle of V.S.O.P. brandy be aged for?
53. How long should a bottle of Napoleon brandy be aged for?
54. Cognac is aged in oak barrels made from oak trees grown in ....?
55. A wine with a higher than the minimum required alcoholic content is known as ....?
56. The most full bodied wine from the Alsace region is ....?
57. What does the term Gewürz indicate?
58. Name the popular spirit produced in the town of Condom?
59. What was Napoleon's favourite wine?
60. Which is the biggest V.D.Q.S. producing area of France?
61. The song "The night they invented champagne" was featured in which film and sung by....?
62. Which wine area is supposedly named after Julius Caesar?
63. Which famous château commissions a famous artist to design the upper portion of its wine label every year?
64. Name three artists who were commissioned for this work.
65. Louis Pasteur was born in which wine region?
66 In 1891 French President Sadi Carnot rode through them in a carriage drawn by white horses. What were they?
67. For the Paris Exhibition of 1889, what did Eugene Mercier commission which took 20 years to build?
68. What emblem is embossed on bottles of Châteauneuf du Pape?

ITALY

1. The term Abboccato indicates ....
2. The term Dolce indicates ....
3. Amabile is an Italian labelling term which refers to ....
4. Is Asti the name of a town, grape variety, or a river?
5. Turin is the centre of which drink?

6. Name two wines from the Piedmont region.
7. Name two wines from the Veneto region.
8. Name Italy's largest wine producing region.
9. Which region produces Sfurzat?
10. Secco on a wine label indicates ....
11. Is Italy the world's largest exporter of wine?
12. The term rosso indicates ....
13. What is grappa?
14. Which region of Italy does not produce wine?
15. The term spumante indicates ....
16. The term Classico on a wine label indicates ....
17. The term Riserva on a wine label indicates ....
18. The term Frizzante on a wine label indicates ....
19. What is the Trebbiano grape named after?
20. Which country is the largest importer of Italian wines?
21. Soave is a wine from which region of Italy?
22. Ciro is produced in which wine region?
23. A black cockerel is on the seal of which Italian wine?
24. A cherub is on the seal of which Italian wine?
25. Where is Monica wine produced?
26. From which region is the wine Faro produced?
27. Where is the liqueur Elixir Di China produced?
28. Which wines carries the distinguished hallmark of Christ under the press?
29. Albana is a wine from which area?
30. What famous wine comes from Liguria?
31. Which grape variety is used in Asti Spumante?
32. Which wine comes from grapes grown on the slopes of the extinct volcano Monte Vulture?
33. Chianti Classico DOCG mainly uses which grape variety?
34. What grape variety is used in the production of Bruno Di Montalciano?
35. The centre of the vermouth trade of Italy is in which city?
36. Italian quality wines have the initials ...... on the label.
37. Which wine is produced from grapes grown on the slopes of Mount Vesuvius?
38. In what year were the DOC wine laws passed?
39. Which wine has a seal depicting the Patron Saint San Secundo on its bottles?
40. Etna is a wine produced in which region?
41. What does the term Cotto indicate?
42. From which region does the wine Rossese di Dolcecqua (sweet water) originate?
43. Lambrusco is produced in which region?
44. Which wine is named after a town dedicated to Janus, the two faced god of Doors?
45. Which grape variety is named after the Italian word for fog (Nebbia)?
46. Chianti Colli Senesi wine label depicts ....
47. Fara is a dry red wine from which region?
48. Name the region which produces Est Est Est di Montefiascone wine.

49. In which region is Orvieto produced?
50. Inferno is a wine produced in which region?

GERMANY

1. Name two great rivers of Europe which flow from one Swiss glazier.
2. What is edelfoule?
3. Does Germany produce red wine?
4. Name three rivers in the wine growing area of Germany other than the Rhine.
5. What is the lowest category of German wine called?
6. What is the highest category of German wine called?
7. In which year did Germany introduce its first wine law?
8. Moselle wines are sold in which colour bottle?
9. Rhine wines are sold in which colour bottle?
10. Liebraumilch wine comes from which German region?
11. What name do the British give to Rhine wines?
12. In which Moselle city was Karl Marx born?
13. The valley of the AHR is noted for which type of wine?
14. Bernkasteler Doktor comes from which wine region?
15. Which German town faces the town of Bingen across the Rhine?
16. Name the famous German brandy produced in this town.
17. What is Rotwein?
18. The wine Blue Nun comes from which wine district?
19. Which legendary jilted heroine lured sailors and fishermen to their doom on the river Rhine?
20. What does the term Trocken indicate?
21. What does the term Bereich indicate?
22. What is Eiswein?
23. What is Oechsle?
24. Is Britain the biggest importer of German wines?
25. Are German wines the most northerly of Europe?
26. What does the term Einzellage mean?
27. What does the word Grosslage mean?
28. What does the word Kabinett mean on the label of QMP wine?
29. What does the word Spätlesee mean on the label of QMP wine?
30. What does the word Auslese mean on the label of QMP wine?
31. What does the word Beerenauslese mean on the label of QMP wine?
32. What does the word Trockenbeerenausle mean on the label of QMP wine?
33. In which area is the largest quantity of German wine produced?
34. In which area is the smallest quantity of German wine produced?
35. What does the word Profungsnummer indicate?
36. Who is the Patron Saint of wine in Germany?
37. The term Sekt indicates ....
38. The term Domane indicates ....

39. How many wine growing regions are there in Germany?
40. Name five regions.
41. What percentage of red wine is produced in Germany?
42. If the name of the grape appears on the wine label, what percentage of the wine must come from that variety?
43. Johannesberg is in which wine region?
44. Cochem is in which wine region?

SPAIN AND PORTUGAL

1. What is sangria?
2. Tinto is the Spanish word for ....
3. The term gran reserva indicates ....
4. What is Flor?
5. Crianza is the name given to ....
6. A bodega is a ....
7. The word cepa means ....
8. What is the Solera system?
9. The following terms Fino, Oloroso, Manzanilla, Amontillado, indicate ....
10. Name the river that flows through Rioja and then into the Mediterranean.
11. Name three wine regions of Spain.
12. Is Tempranillo the main grape variety used in the production of sherry?
13. Rayas could be described as ....
14. The Spanish name for a wine cellar is ....
15. Criadera is a word used to describe ....
16. Name the three main types of sherry.
17. Name a red wine, a white wine and a sparkling wine from Spain.
18. From which region does the white wine Alba Flora originate?
19. Sherry is named after which Spanish town?
20. What grape variety shares its name with a horse?
21. Name two vines used in the production of Madeira.
22. Name two vines used in the production of Port.
23. What is Estufa?
24. What are Quintas?
25. What are Lagares?
26. How many distinctive styles of port are there?
27. Reserva on the label of a bottled Spanish wine indicates ....
28. Gran Reserva on the label of a bottled Spanish wine indicates ....
29. Name one white wine and one red wine from Navarra.
30. Which region gave the name amontillado to sherry?
31. The term sercial on a label of Madeira wine indicates ....
32. The term verdelho on a label of Madeira wine indicates ....
33. The term Bual on a label of Madeira wine indicates ....

34. The term Malmsey on a label of Madeira wine indicates ....
35. Which wine region of Portugal was immune from the ravages of Plylloxera owing to the depth of its sandy soil?
36. Which area used to be famous for a coarse sweet red wine named Red Biddy?
37. Who drowned himself in a butt of Malmsey wine while imprisoned in the Bloody Tower?
38. Vinhosverdes is a wine from which area of Portugal?
39. Name a Portuguese wine of three letters.
40. Is Bairrada wine named after a town, grape variety, soil or river?
41. What was the Metheum Treaty?
42. Name the major countries which produce cork.

SPARKLING WINE

1. Name the world's most famous sparkling wine.
2. A Jeroboam contains .... bottles of champagne.
3. A double bottle of champagne is called ....
4. What percentage of black grapes are used to make champagne?
5. Name the grape varieties used to make champagne.
6. What temperature should champagne be served?
7. Champagne made with only white grapes is known as ....
8. What is vintage champagne?
9. What is non vintage champagne?
10. How many stages of fermentation is there in the production of champagne?
11. Name two towns in the champagne area.
12. The term "méthode champenoise" means ....
13. How is sediment removed from champagne?
14. The term dosage means ....
15. What does the word crémant indicate?
16. Name six of the top producers of champagne.
17. The letters N.V. on a champagne bottle indicates ....
18. Sir Winston Churchill was associated with which champagne?
19. Frizzante on a wine label indicates ....
20. Which nation is the world's largest consumer of sparkling wine per head of population?
21. Name an Italian sparkling wine
22. Name a Spanish sparkling wine
23. Other than champagne name two other sparkling wines from France.
24. The best glass for serving sparkling wine is ....
25. Who said "Why do I drink champagne for breakfast - doesn't everyone?"
26. What is the atmospheric pressure in a bottle of champagne?
27. Name one of the rivers which flow through the champagne area.
28. Very dry champagne is called ....
29. Sweet champagne is indicated on the label as ....
30. The German word spritzig indicates ....

31. The soil in the champagne area is mainly ....
32. Is red wine produced in champagne?
33. To which order of monks did Dom Pérignon belong?
34. Who invented remuage?
35. Which champagne house is the largest shipper of champagne?
36. The labels of the champagne sent to England after whose death were bordered in black?
37. How long should you keep champagne?
38. How should you cool champagne?
39. What are the three methods of making sparkling wine?
40. Is there such a wine as still champagne?
41. By law what must all champagne corks have printed on them?
42. What is pink champagne?
43. A Rehoboam contains how many bottles?
44. A Balthazar contains how many bottles?
45. A Salmanazar contains how many bottles?
46. A Methuselah contains how many bottles?
47. What is tete de cuvée?
48. What is champagne cider?
49. What is a Black Velvet?
50. Who was Champagne Charlie?
51. Vouvray is a sparkling wine from which region?
52. A Nebuchadnezzar contains how many bottles?
53. Which is the quickest and cheapest method of producing a sparkling wine?
54. The metal clasp which holds the champagne cork in place is called ....
55. Who is the "chef de cave"?
56. Why must care be taken to ensure that the black grapes are not over ripe?
57. Who had his boots polished with champagne?
58. Who said champagne was "the best ever hangover cure"?
59. M.A. This code on a Champagne label indicates ....
60. What does the code R.M. on a Champagne label indicate?
61. What does the code N.M. on a Champagne label indicate?
62. This winner of the English Grand National was named after which Champagne House?

TRUE OR FALSE?

1. All brandy is cognac.
2. All cognac is brandy.
3. Sassicaia is a red wine from Italy.
4. Wines aged longer in casks are called Riserva.
5. Bushmills is the oldest legal distillery in the world.
6. Châteauneuf de Pape is produced in the Vatican.
7. The South of France produces 15% of the total volume of Vin de Pays wines.
8. About 10% of all Vin de Pays wines are white.

9. Carmel Avdat is an Israeli white wine.
10. Breathing time is essential for wines.
11. Margaret River is in New Zealand.
12. The spirit Arrack is made from dates.
13. The spirit Tequila is made from Cactus.
14. All Saints is a vineyard in New Zealand.
15. Anjou is a sparkling wine from Portugal.
16. The drink associated at the opening of a meal is called an Aperitif.
17. Côte is the French word for slope or side of hill.
18. Cru refers to a vineyard of quality or growth.
19. Cuve refers to contents of a vat.
20. Cuvée refers to a vat.
21. Grand Cru refers to a great growth.
22. The Hennessey brandy firm was founded by a Scotsman.
23. Legs refer to trails that run down the side of a wine glass after the wine has been swirled around.
24. Canadian Whiskey is spelt with an 'e'.
25. Ernest Hemmingway named his daughter after a French wine.
26. Negotiant is a shipper.
27. Did Louis Noilly bring a Prat into his business?
28. The town of Midleton produces Scotch Whisky.
29. Potheen is a legally produced spirit.
30. Scarlett O'Hara is a cocktail.
31. France is the largest producer of wine.
32. The higher the PH figure the less acid content.
33. Ullage is the name given to the conversion of sugars into alcohol.
34. Sangria is sherry mixed with white wine.
35. Mexico is ranked 20th in the world wine production.
36. Mascara is a wine district.
37. The Bay of Plenty is in California.
38. The Valley of Plenty is in Australia.
39. The Valley of the Moon is in Sonoma Country.
40. Serve all drinks from the left.
41. Robert Louis Stevenson honeymooned in the Napa valley.
42. Rainwater is a wine from California.
43. Sake is produced from barley.
44. The best Cognac comes from low quality wines.
45. Clos is the name given to a plot of land enclosed by a wall.
46. Blanc de Noirs indicates white wine from black grapes.
47. Beaujolais is made from Pinot Noir.
48. Cuvée Close refers to the method of making sparkling wine in a sealed vat.
49. Commanderia St. John is a wine which uses herbs as an infusion.
50. Christian Brothers own the largest winery in the Napa Valley.

51. A vicar patented the first corkscrew in 1795.
52. Argentina is the fourth largest wine producer in the world.
53. Lacryma Christi wine translated means "tears of Christ".
54. Armagnac is produced in the area of "Gers".
55. The grain used in Canadian Whisky is barley.
56. Marsala is a fortified wine from Madeira.
57. The mistral is a river which flows through Alsace.
58. The alcoholic strength of Châteauneuf de Pape must never be less than 8% when sold.
59. Provence is famous as the home of Napoleon.
60. Kirsch is distilled from the fermented juice of plums.
61. Less than 30% of white grapes are used to make champagne.
62. Spain is the second largest producer of wine in the world.
63. Red wines are produced in Majorca.
64. Malaga is a fortified wine.
65. An Englishman invented Marsala.
66. The nebbiolo is the principal grape variety used in the production of Rioja.
67. The alcoholic content of fortified wines is 25-30 degrees.
68. Port can be both red and white.
69. In the E.C. can a sparkling wine be legally called champagne other than from the legally controlled champagne area of France?
70. Wine used in the Roman Catholic Mass must be made entirely from grape must.
71. Port can only be made in the Douro Region.
72. Wines of fitou are usually white.
73. Potential alcoholic strength can be measured by using a refractometer.
74. Highland malts are separated from lowland malts by an imaginary line which runs from Dundee to Greenock.
75. Dom Perignon experimented on clarification and sparkle at the Abbey of Rheims.
76. Soave is a dry wine from Tuscany.
77. Wines which have been fortified have had Spirit added.
78. Vines will produce better quality grapes for wine making if they are grown on slopes facing east.
79. The French wine making region closest to the German border is Savoie.
80. The most northerly district in Burgundy is called Côte Maconnaise.
81. When serving wine the bottle should be twisted to avoid drips.
82. A bottle of wine is presented to the host so that he can verify his choice.
83. Red wine will keep longer the higher the tannin content.
84. Saumur is correctly described as a sparkling wine from Touraine.
85. Muscadet is correctly described as sparkling wine from the Loire.
86. Malborough is a wine producing region of England.
87. Minervois is a wine producing region of Languedoc.
88. Tonic water contains quinine.
89. Côte Rôtie is a red wine produced in Medoc.
90. Piesporter is a wine producing area in Alsace.

91. Apollinaris is a natural mineral water from Germany.
92. Hawkes Bay is a vineyard in New Zealand.
93. Château Petrus is produced in Pomerol.
94. Barolo is a red wine from Umbria.
95. Bairrada is a red wine from Spain.
96. Chinon is a red wine from the Loire.
97. Vin Doux is a sweet fortified wine.
98. Strega is bright yellow in colour.
99. The Chardonnay grape variety is common in Alsace.
100. A White Lady contains fresh orange juice.
101. Metaxa is a brandy produced in Holland.
102. The city of Cork was famous for its production of cork.
103. The river Rhône flows into the Mediterranean.
104. Tequila gets its name from a town in Mexico.
105. Whiskey is not produced in Japan.
106. Iskra is a sparkling wine from Greece.
107. Marthas vineyard produces wine.
108. Italy is the largest importer of champagne.
109. Kissadee is a white rum produced in Ireland.
110. Raki is a Turkish aniseed flavoured liqueur.
111. Barbaresco and Barbera are both grape varieties.
112. Bingen is situated on the River Rhine and River Nahe.
113. Loess is a soil constituent.
114. Manseng is a grape variety.
115. Quincy is a wine area of Provence.
116. Bourgueil is a white wine from the Loire.
117. Fronsac, Bourg and Blaye are all red wine districts.
118. Classic Sauternes grapes are picked individually.
119. Domaine de Chevalier is situated in Bordeaux.
120. Tarragona dessert wine is sometimes known as 'poor mans port'.
121. Puszta is an aperitif containing apricot brandy and sweet Tokaji wine.

DRINK - HEALTH AND LEGAL

1. What allowances of alcohol can we bring home from Europe without paying any UK duty or VAT (applies to duty and VAT having been paid in the country where the drink was purchased)?
2. What is the legal limit of alcohol in 100ml of breath?
3. What is the legal limit of alcohol per 100ml of urine?
4. Are restaurants legally obliged to serve tap water or can they refuse?
5. How many molicules of water are needed to break down one molicule of alcohol?
6. For most people it takes about .... hours for the liver to reduce blood alcohol by about 12mg/100ml.

7. How many calories are there in a single unit of alcohol?
8. Alcohol passes easily from a Mother's bloodstream into her unborn baby. True or False?
9. The concentration of alcohol in your body depends on what?
10. How long does it take the body to get rid of the alcohol in two pints of beer?
11. Having an alcoholic drink warms you up. True or False?
12. What are the penalties if convicted of drink driving?
13. It is illegal to give a child alcohol under what age?
14. What are the social consequences if convicted of drink driving?
15. What are the financial consequences if convicted of drink driving?
16. What is a long pull?
17. What are the normal duty free and VAT free allowance limits for alcoholic drinks when entering the UK?
18. What new regulations were introduced in 1993 regarding duty free allowances when travelling between EC countries?
19. Do spirits contain any minerals or vitamins?
20. Which European country has the legal limit of 20mg alcohol per 100ml of breath?
21. Which European country has the legal limit of 40mg alcohol per 100ml of breath?
22. What is the children's certificate allowing children into pubs?
23. What are the three broad guidelines set out by the government for granting a children's certificate?
24. What is the daily allowance of alcoholic drink for junior ratings on board British warships?
25. When was the rum rations for junior ratings on British warships abolished?
26. What are the duty free allowances for alcohol in the Irish Republic (applies to duty and VAT already been paid in the EEC country where purchased)?

KEEPING A CHECK ON YOUR DRINKING

Medical experts advise that 21 units for a man and 15 units for a woman spread evenly throughout the week is unlikely to damage their health. Above these levels there is a potential health risk. One unit of alcohol is equivalent to half a pint of Beer, 125ml Wine, 50ml Port/Sherry or 25ml Spirits. It is best not to drink alcohol whilst you are taking prescribed medication.
Drinking and driving do not mix, take a taxi. One unit of alcohol contains approximately 100 calories. Do not do DIY jobs after drinking. Keep drink secure from children and avoid alcohol prior to sport and especially before swimming. To maintain a general level of health and fitness control your drinking. There are obvious differences between the sensory pleasures and health benefits of moderate and responsible consumption of drink, and the potential dangers that abuse and misuse of alcohol can create.

N.B.

From midnight on June 30th 1999, travellers moving between E U countries will not be able to purchase duty free goods. Only travel outside the E U would still carry duty-free benefits.

Drink Teasers

Grape Varieties

Given below are the names of some varieties of grapes which have been jumbled up.

Write beneath each the correct name.

1 IRON TONPI

2 GYAMA

3 CNNARDOAHY

4 NEOLOBIB

5 PAMINOOL

6 SRAZIH

7 PITON MNIREUE

8 ZIDELFAN

9 GINLSEIR

10 TOLREM

11 CANETREB RANFC

12 TRANOEBBI

13 TELINAMPRLO

14 BRABREA

15 CABTENRE VSINAGUNO

16 MILLONSE

17 SANONGIVU LCABN

18 NCHNEI LNCAB

19 GHENERAC

20 CITLAUNS

21 SRENVILA

22 MURELL RUGTAHU

23 AETOGIL

24 VIREINGO

25 MASIAAVL

Wine Anagrams

Sort out the anagrams to make the name of a wine.

There is one extra letter in each line which can be used to make another wine reated word from each group

	JUMBLED	CORRECT WORD	EXTRA LETTER	NEW WORD
1	CARNOGC	______	____	
	AOVSES	______	____	
	ALGAMEA	______	____	
	CAMOUN	______	____	
	TARETCIL	______	____	
	PITHANCI	______	____	______
2	MALOCNIPO	______	____	
	LOCNAM	______	____	
	WAEINESE	______	____	
	EOAD	______	____	
	BIHLTSC	______	____	
	SADNOGIGR	______	____	______
3	AHEVLT	______	____	
	MURSYAU	______	____	
	ARAMSRAL	______	____	
	NIXIFA	______	____	
	CADMUSSTE	______	____	______
4	RLOMEPRO	______	____	
	LOYYANV	______	____	
	AAGSALM	______	____	
	RAHMDEIA	______	____	
	SALERAMA	______	____	
	ARAGROTRAN	______	____	______
5	RSEBMUAUTL	______	____	
	RUARESNEC	______	____	
	ORNNHIC	______	____	
	LOGBNDA	______	____	
	NYUSTEANA	______	____	
	LYNABE	______	____	
	DLERULY	______	____	
	YLMOES	______	____	______
6	RSABREBA	______	____	
	VRYOAUVI	______	____	
	NIENCRDOU	______	____	
	VESAOV	______	____	
	TUAFOI	______	____	______

Wine Words

Can you fill in the missing spaces?

STYLE	France	Italy	Spain	Germany	Portugal	Yugoslavia	Hungary
White	Blanc					Bijelo	Feher
Red		Rosso				Crno	Voros
Sparkling			Espumoso			Biser	Habzo
Dry				Trocen		Suho	Szaraz
Sweet					Doce	Slatko	Edes
Rosé						Ruzica	

Odd One Out

Each group of words has one word out of place, which one does not belong and why?

St Émilion	St Estèphe	St Julien	St Péray
Anjou	Tavel	Mateus	Touraine
Grappa	Cognac	Marc	Aguardiente
Curacao	Calvados	Grand Marnier	Cointreau
Pomerol	Fronsac	St Émilion	Morgon
Bougeuil	Cornas	Hermitage	Gigondas
Bahai	Kahlua	Tia Maria	Sambuca
Malmsey	Bual	Sercial	Marsala
Fino	Tawny	Amontillado	Manzanilla
Pinot Noir	Chardonnay	Shiraz	Gamay
Minervois	Malmsey	Macon	Montrachet
Pernod	Ouzo	Pastis	Ricard
Evian	Vittel	Perrier	Contrexeville
Fraise	Framboise	Grenadine	Gomme
Fleurie	Brouilly	Chenas	Barsac
Gironde	Garonne	Saone	Dordogne
Bardolino	Soave	Valpolicella	Orvieto
Penedes	Valdepenas	Montilla	Bairrada
Asti Spumante	Bardolino	Chianti	Orvieto

Rivers of Wine

Write in the space provided the wine regions where the rivers listed flow.

RIVER	REGION/COUNTRY
MURRAY	____________________
DARLING	____________________
HUDSON	____________________
COLUMBIA	____________________
SANTA MARGARITA	____________________
ESTRELLA	____________________
SALINAS	____________________
RUSSIAN	____________________
MOULOUYA	____________________
OSAM	____________________
MURA	____________________
OHRE	____________________
DOURO	____________________
RIO LIMA	____________________
FRANCOLI	____________________
EBRO	____________________
SACCO	____________________
TEVERE	____________________
LIESER	____________________
GOLO	____________________
ISERE	____________________
DOUBS	____________________
TET	____________________
WEISS	____________________
GOULBURN	____________________
LAHN	____________________
BODROG	____________________
MARCIA	____________________
DROPT	____________________
PO	____________________
TARA	____________________
BAISE	____________________
OJA	____________________

Wine and Song

HOW MANY SONGS/MUSIC CAN YOU NAME WITH A DRINK IN THE TITLE?

Cocktails

NAME THE INGREDIENTS IN THE COCKTAILS LISTED BELOW:

BETWEEN THE SHEETS ______________________
BUCKS FIZZ ______________________
BLUE LADY ______________________
BRONX ______________________
BROOKLYN ______________________
CHOCOLATE SOLDIER ______________________
DAIQUIRI ______________________
FIRST NIGHT ______________________
GIN AND IT ______________________
GRAND SLAM ______________________
HARVEY WALLBANGER ______________________
HONEYMOON ______________________
LONDON FOG ______________________
MAIDENS PRAYER ______________________
MANHATTEN ______________________
MAPLE LEAF ______________________
PARADISE ______________________
PINK LADY ______________________
RUSTY NAIL ______________________
SAN FRANCISCO ______________________
WHITE LADY ______________________
SHIRLEY TEMPLE/ROY ROGERS ______________________
JUMP UP AND KISS ME ______________________

Speciality Coffees

NAME THE SPIRIT IN THE COFFEES LISTED:

MONKS ______________________
GAELIC ______________________
SEVILLE ______________________
RUSSIAN ______________________
MEXICAN ______________________
FRENCH ______________________
JAMAICAN ______________________
CALYPSO ______________________
WITCHES ______________________
KENTUCKY ______________________
MISSISSIPPI ______________________
FLAMENCO ______________________
BONNIE PRINCE CHARLIE ______________________
SCOTCH MIST ______________________
HIGHLANDER ______________________

Where do they come from?

Simply write in the space provided the region in France from which the following wines originate.

	WINES	REGIONS
1.	GIGONDAS	________________
2.	BANDOL	________________
3.	BOUZY	________________
4.	SANCERRE	________________
5.	MUSCADET	________________
6.	VOUGEOT	________________
7.	VOSNE-ROMANÉE	________________
8.	GEWÜRZTRAMINER	________________
9.	BARSAC	________________
10.	FRONSAC	________________
11.	A C CASSIS	________________
12.	FITOU	________________
13.	FLEURIE	________________
14.	VOLNAY	________________
15.	ANJOU	________________
16.	CONDRIEU	________________
17.	TAVEL	________________
18.	MONBAZILLAC	________________
19.	BOURG	________________
20.	SAUTERNES	________________
21.	CORBIERES	________________
22.	CHINON	________________
23.	BELLET	________________
24.	ARBOIS PUPILLIN	________________
25.	CHÂTEAUNEUF-DU-PAPE	________________

What do you know about liqueurs?

What are the flavours and from which countries do each of the liqueurs originate?

	LIQUEUR	**FLAVOUR and COUNTRY**
1.	OUZO	____________
2.	SABRA	____________
3.	TIA MARIA	____________
4.	BAILEYS IRISH CREAM	____________
5.	CRÊME DE KIRSCH	____________
6.	CHARTREUSE	____________
7.	ADVOCAAT	____________
8.	AMARETTO	____________
9.	SOUTHERN COMFORT	____________
10.	GALLIANO	____________
11.	CURACAO	____________
12.	IRISH MIST	____________
13.	DRAMBUIE	____________
14.	BENEDICTINE D O M	____________
15.	SAMBUCA	____________
16.	IZZARA	____________
17.	BRONTE	____________
18.	CASSIS	____________
19.	PARFAIT AMOUR	____________
20.	KUMMEL	____________
21.	COINTREAU	____________
22.	MIDORI	____________
23.	BAHIA	____________
24.	EDELWEISS	____________
25.	GLAYVA	____________
26.	MIRABELLE	____________
27.	AURUM	____________
28.	GRAND MARNIER	____________
29.	MARASCHINO	____________
30.	VAN DER HUM	____________

How good are you on Italian Wines?

All you have to do is to match the wines listed below with the region of origin. To make it easy, listed at the foot of the page are the wine regions of Italy.

	WINES	REGION
1.	FRASCATI	____________
2.	CHIANTI	____________
3.	BAROLO	____________
4.	MARSALA	____________
5.	VERDICCHIO DEI CASTELLI DI JESI	____________
6.	SOAVE	____________
7.	VALPOLICELLA	____________
8.	EST EST EST	____________
9.	ETNA ROSSO	____________
10.	ORVIETO	____________
11.	BARDOLINO	____________
12.	ISCHIA BIANCO	____________
13.	SASSELLA	____________
14.	LAMBRUSCO	____________
15.	NEBBIOLA D'ALBA	____________
16.	BARBARESCO	____________
17.	AMARONE	____________
18.	BARBERA D'ASTI	____________
19.	LACRYMA CHRISTI	____________
20.	FALERNO	____________
21.	CIRO	____________
22.	ALCAMO	____________
23.	ASTI SPUMANTE	____________
24.	CINQUE TERRE	____________
25.	CASTEL DEL MONTE	____________

WINE REGIONS

PIEDMONT	LATIUM	VENETO
SICILIY	LIGURIA	APULIA
CALABRIA	EMILIA ROMAGNA	CAMPANIA
TUSCANY	SARDINIA	LOMBARDY
UMBRIA	TRENTO ALTO-ADIGE	FRIULI-VENEZIA-GIULIA
MARCHES	VAL D'AOSTA	ABRUZZO

Who said what about Drink?

1. "I'm only a beer teetotaller not a Champagne teetotaller."
2. "In victory you deserve it, in defeat you need it."
3. "Champagne is the healthiest and most hygienic."
4. "Only people without imagination cannot find a good reason for not drinking Champagne."
5. "If the aunt of the vicar has never touched liquor look out when she finds the Champagne"
6. "Champagne is funny stuff. I'm used to whiskey. Whiskey is a slap on the back and Champagne mist before the eyes."
7. "Champagne - Ah. There's a certain .... love about it. I always drink it with a new woman."
8. "Claret is for the boys. Port is for the men, but Cognac is a drink for heroes."
9. "Who loves not wine, women and song remains a fool his whole life long."
10. "Let me have wine and women, mirth and laughter. Sermons the day after."
11. "The wine is bottled poetry."
12. The problem is that many MPs never see the London that exists beyond the wine bars and brothels of Westminster."
13. "Dinner at the Huntercombe's possessed only two dramatic features - the wine was a farce and the food a tragedy."
14. "Happiness is a wine of the rarest vintage and seems insipid to a vulgar taste."
15. "What is man when you come to think of him, but a minutely set ingenious machine for turning with artfulness the red wine of Shiraz into urine."
16. "Wine and wenches empty mens purses."
17. "I may not here omit those two main plagues and common dotages of human kind wine and women which have infatuated and besotted myriads of people. They go commonly together."
18. "The older I become, sir, the more I value your kindness. Your excellent wine is becoming indispensable to me."
19. "Wine is the first weapon that devils use."
20. "Whisky to a Scotsman is as innocent as milk is to the rest of the human race."
21. From the bonny bells of heather, they brewed a drink lang syne, Was sweeter than honey, was stronger than wine.
22. "The King of drinks as I conceive it TALISKER, ISLAY OR GLENLIVET."
23. "Let us toast John Barleycorn, each man a glass in hand
And may his greater prosperity ne'er fail in old Scotland."
24. Le goot duvin n'est pas un crime et il en fait rarement commettre les buveurs ont de la cordial de la francais ils sont presque tous bons.
25. Pour le vin il n'y pas de terme fixe mais ne bois pas jusqua l'ivresse.
26. Le vin allume lesyeux chauffe la bouche, enflamme le corps embrase le coeur et fait 'etinceler l'esprit.
27. Bien fou quin'aime pas boire car le vin nous remplit d'une voluptueuse iuresse le vin nous invite a'la danse, et nous fait oublier nos maux.
28. Ah! Qu'un verre de vin serait le bienvenue. a juin moi j'ai l'esprit reveur et saugremi
Je bois in coup lerreir s'en VQ je faux se brise avez vous remanque cela le vin degrise.

29. I drink Champagne when I am happy and when I am sad. Sometimes I drink it when I'm alone. When I have company I consider it obligatory. I trifle with it if I'm not hungry and drink it when I am. Otherwise I never touch it - unless I'm thirsty.
30. Man who drink too much, think little.
31. For the best way to open conversation, use corkscrew.
32. Girl who drink to much beer soon begin to feel little 'run down'.
33. Whiskey sometimes make one feel like new person, but soon make look like old one.
34. I would be quite happy to see the devil's buttermilk banned from society.
35. Freedom and whisky gang the gither.

What drink is used in the following dishes?

	DISH	DRINK USED
1.	TRIFLE AUX XERES	______________
2.	ZABAGLIONE	______________
3.	CRÊPE SUZETTE	______________
4.	COUPE JAMAIQUE	______________
5.	BOMBE AIDA	______________
6.	COUPE ANDALOUSE	______________
7.	BOMBE CLICQUOT	______________
8.	COUPE ELIZABETH	______________
9.	COUPE EUGENE	______________
10.	ZUCCOTTO	______________
11.	TIRAMISU	______________
12.	SOUFFLE GRAND MARNIER	______________
13.	BAKED ALASKA	______________
14.	FLUMMERY	______________
15.	TRIPE A LA CAEN	______________
16.	TOURNEDO ROSSINI	______________
17.	CHICKEN CHASSEUR	______________
18.	ENTRECOTE MARCHAND DE VIN	______________
19.	WELSH RAREBIT	______________
20.	CARBONNADE OF BEEF	______________
21.	LOBSTER BISQUE	______________
22.	FONDUE	______________
23.	LEMON POSSET	______________
24.	BANANA FLAMBE	______________
25.	STEAK DIANE	______________
26.	TURTLE SOUP	______________
27.	STRAWBERRIES ROMANOFF	______________
28.	SCAMPI PROVENCALE	______________
29.	LOBSTER THERMIDOR	______________
30.	BEEF BOURGUIGNONNE	______________
31.	ATHOL BROSE	______________

Proverb, Toast and Saying Teasers

Break the code and solve the following:

1. QPSU JT UIF DVSF GPS BMM JMMT FYDFQU EFBUI — Portugese
2. XJOF SFWFBMT VIF USVUI — Irish
3. XIBU CVUUFS PS XIJTLFZ XJMM OPU DVSF UIFSFT OP DVSF GPS — Irish
4. UIF XJOF PG CVSHVOEZ NBLFT UIF XIPMF ESJOL UP UIF IFBMUI PG GSBODF — French
5. “PO TU NBSUJOT EBZ XJOUFS JT DMPTJOH JO” — French
6. “BGUFS TU WJODFOUT EBZ XF DBO TUBSU QSVOJOH” — French
7. FBTFUS FBSMZ PS FBTFUS MBUF UIF TIPPUT EPOU XBJU — French
8. “BVHVTU NBLFT UIF XJOF, TFQUFNCFS UIF IBSWFTU. JO UIFTF UXP NPOUIT FWFSZUIJOH HPFT XFMM” — French
9. “PG BMM BHSJDVMUVSBM MBCPVST UIFSF JT OPOF IBSEFS UIBO UIBU PG UIBU PG UIF XJOF HSPXFS. CFOU BMNPTU UP UIF HSPVOE,
TRVBUUJOH XJUI IJT LOFFT BQBSU PWFS UIF VOZJFMEJOH FBSUI,
UIF NBO IBE UP CSFBL VQ
UIF JSPO-IBSE DMPET XJUI IJT TIPSU
QJDL-BYF BOE SFNPWF BMM UIF TUOFT UIFSF GSPN. BMM UIJT
CBDL-CSFBLJOH UPJM IBE UP CF BDDPNQMJTIFE JO UIF TQBDF PG
B TJOHMF TFBTPO” — French
10. BGUFS NFMPO XJOF JT B GFMPO
11. GFBTUJOH JT UIF QIZTJDJBOT IBSWFTU
12. CBDDIVT IBT ESPXOFE NPSF NFO UIBO OFQUVOF
13. ESVOLFOFTT NBLFT TPNF NFO GPPMT, TPNF CFBTUT BOE TPNF EFWJMT
14. B XPNBO UIBU MPWFT UP CF BU UIF XJOEPX JT MJLF B CVODI PG HSBQFT PO UIF IJHIXBZ
15. NBZ UIF SPPG PG ZPVS IPVTF OFWFS GBMM JO BOE UIPTF XJUIJO OFWFS GBMM PVU
16. H PPE GPS UIF MJWFS NBZ CF CBE GPS UIF TQMFFO
17. QPFUSZ JT EFWJMT XJOF
18. H PE EFQSJWFT IJN PG CSFBE XIP MJLFT OPU IJT ESJOL
19. NBZ ZPV CF JO IFBWFO B IBMG IPVS CFGPSF UIF EFWJM LOPX ZPVS EFBE
20. QSJEF CSFBLGBTUFE XJUIQMFOUZ, EJOFE XJUI QPWFSUZ BOE TVQQFE XJUI JOGBNZ
21. ESJOL MFTT BU MVODI MFTT BU EJOOFS TMFFQ BMPGU BOE ZPV XJJ TMFFQ PGU

Polybius Squares

	1	2	3	4	5
1	A	B	C	D	E
2	F	G	H	IJ	K
3	L	M	N	O	P
4	Q	R	S	T	U
5	V	W	X	Y	Z

THIS CIPHER CONVERTS EACH LETTER OF THE ALPHABET INTO A TWO DIGIT NUMBER USING ONLY THE DIGITS 1-5. THE LETTERS I AND J HAVE BEEN PLACED INTO ONE SQUARE SO THAT ALL 26 LETTERS OF THE ENGLISH ALPHABET CAN BE USED IN THE SQUARE GRID.

EXAMPLE

PLAIN TEXT	G	O	O	D		N	I	G	H	T
CRYTOGRAM	22,	34,	34,	14,		33,	24,	22,	23,	44.

WINES TO DECIPHER

1.	13,	23,	24,	33,	34,	33.			
2.	21,	42,	11,	43,	13,	11,	44,	24.	
3.	13,	23,	24,	11,	33,	44,	24		
4.	12,	11,	42.	34,	31,	34.			
5.	42,	24,	15,	43,	31,	24,	33,	22.	
6.	32,	34,	42,	22,	34,	33.			
7.	21.	24,	53,	24,	33.				
8.	22,	11,	32,	11,	54.				
9.	15,	43,	44,	15,	43,	44,	15,	43,	44.
10.	13,	23,	11,	32,	35,	11,	22,	33,	15.

LIQUERS TO DECIPHER

	1	2	3	4	5
1	A	B	C	D	E
2	F	G	H	I	J
3	K	L	M	N	O
4	P	Q	R	S	T
5	U	V	W	X	YZ

1.	22,	43,	11,	34,	14,		33,	11,	43,	34,	24,	15,	43.		
2.	24,	43,	24,	44,	23,		33,	24,	44,	45.					
3.	13,	51,	43,	11,	13,	11,	35.								
4.	31,	11,	23,	32,	51,	11.									
5.	31,	51,	33,	33,	15,	32.									
6.	44,	45,	43,	15,	22,	11.									
7.	45,	24,	11,	33,	11,	43,	24,	11.							
8.	33,	11,	43,	11,	44,	13,	23,	24,	34,	35.					
9.	14,	43,	11,	33,	12,	51,	24,	15.							
10.	13,	43,	15,	33,	15,		14,	15,		33,	15,	34,	45,	23,	15.

Key Number Ciphers

THIS TYPE OF CIPHER USES A KEY NUMBER TO ARRANGE THE COLUMNS IN THE RECTANGLE. IF YOU KNOW THE KEY NUMBER LABEL THE GRID WITH IT AND ENTER THE LETTER GROUPS OF THE ENCIPHERED MESSAGE INTO THE COLUMNS IN THE CORRECT NUMERICAL ORDER.

THE CRYPTOGRAM CAN THEN BE READ HORIZONTALLY.

TO ASSIST YOU THE KEY NUMBER FOR THE FIRST SET OF PROBLEMS IS 24513.

PROBLEMS TO SOLVE

(A)	VWIM	SRNH	EITE	EEEG	RDWA
(B)	OEYR	FSYH	IRSY	IADE	NVRR
(C)	TDOA	PSIT	IERL	OMNU	RAPG
(D)	KZOI	BFSK	SICL	UIAT	CZCA
(E)	NIDO	GEGO	NSFU	USOR	ISOY
(F)	PURL	ASRO	IABE	NATT	IQET
(G)	NAEN	CCED	ABRK	OITR	GSTI
(H)	NANN	CEEO	GTTE	HDRW	AWII

A

2	4	5	1	3

B

2	4	5	1	3

C

2	4	5	1	3

D

2	4	5	1	3

E

2	4	5	1	3

F

2	4	5	1	3

G

2	4	5	1	3

H

2	4	5	1	3

FOR THE SECOND SET OF PROBLEMS TO SOLVE FIRST YOU MUST FIND THE KEY NUMBER.

(I)	IYTPN	IOWOY	WSSTP	ELEAE	NNEHM
(J)	APCSY	AAODC	MLREI	SSUNL	RIDII
(K)	OONME	IATCA	KYNSP	RCIAN	RLAHG
(L)	GNCTN	TMWIL	SASHA	EATIA	REINI
(M)	XBYMO	EIARX	MARFE	OADMC	TSNOI
(N)	CRAUE	OAONN	TWCII	IETQN	NTNSI
(O)	NNSOS	MMAWT	AUTTT	GONBE	ACIOL
(P)	SWRRL	ARNMU	DAIOT	IDFOA	OEEPG

I

J

K

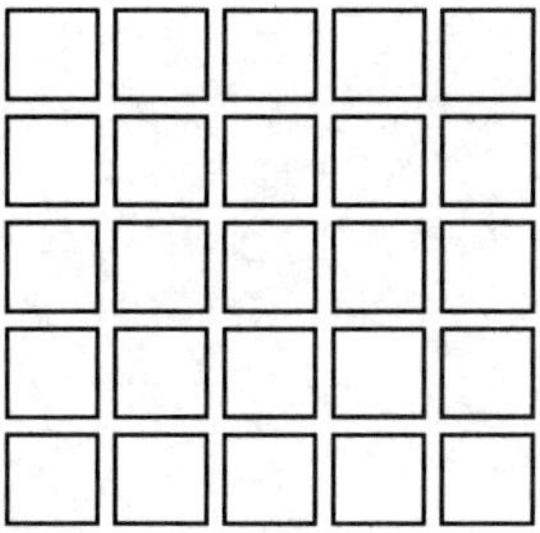

L

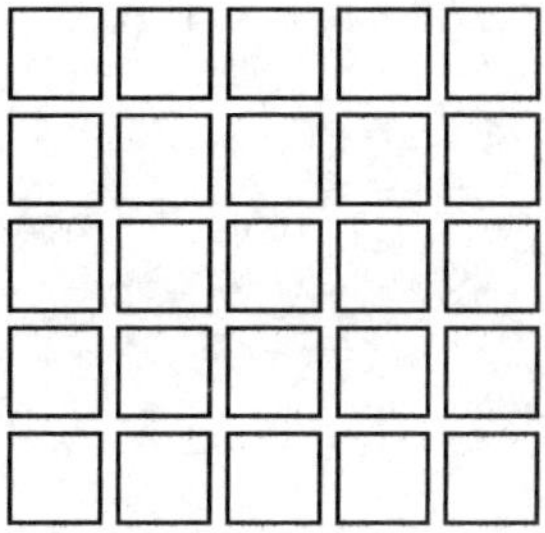

M

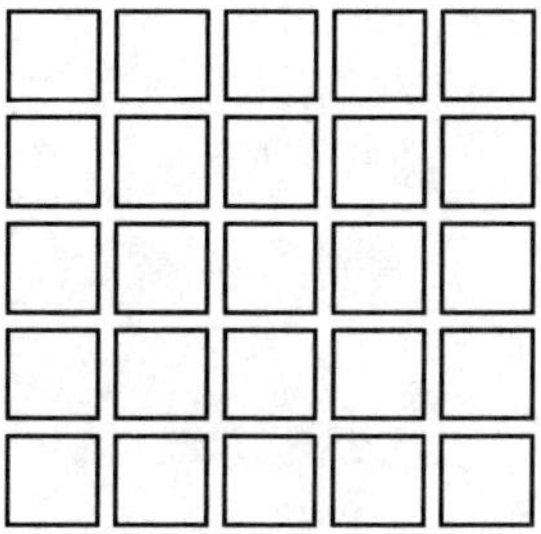

N

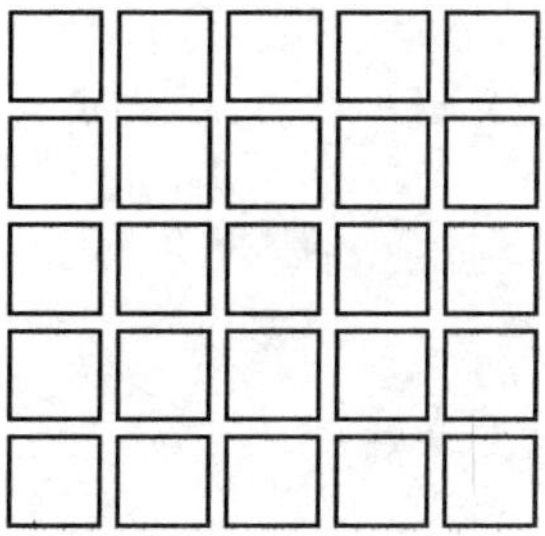

O

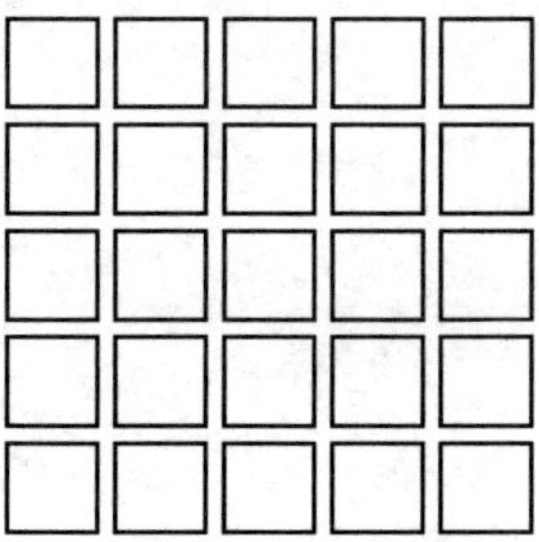

P

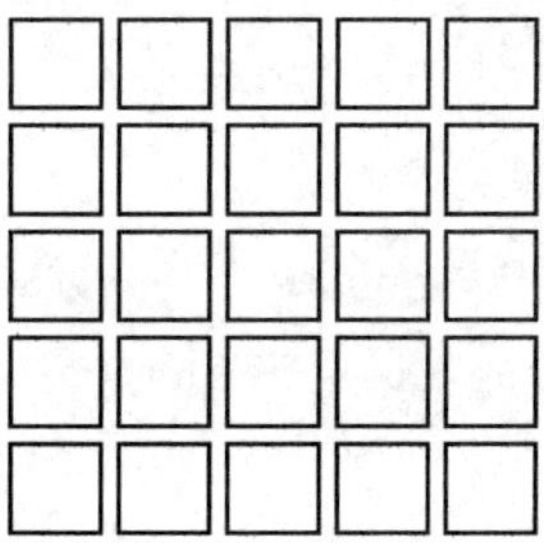

PROVERBS AND SAYINGS

1. Wine reveals the truth.
2. Thirst begets thirst.
3. Sweet is the wine but sours the payment.
4. It's the first drop that destroyed me, there's no harm at all in the last.
5. The cure of drinking is to drink again.
6. When good luck comes the drink comes.
7. Three things a man should not boast of: the size of his purse, the beauty of his wife and the sweetness of his beer.
8. Three things that relate to drink: to drink it, to pay for it and to carry it.
9. Rhineland is wineland.
10. After melon, wine is felon.
11. White meat, white wine, red meat, red wine.
12. All wine would be port if it could.
13. Wine has two defects, if you add water to it you ruin it; if you do not add water to it, it ruins you.
14. Wine lets no lover unrewarded go.
15. The best use of a bad wine is to drive away poor relations.
16. If you come up in this world you never go down in the next.
17. Drink is the curse of the land, it makes you fight with your neighbour, it makes you shoot at your landlord and makes you miss him.
18. What butter and whisky won't cure, there's no cure for.
19. A narrow neck keeps the bottle from being emptied in one swig.
20. Burgundy for Kings, Champagne for Duchesses and Claret for Gentlemen.
21. Water is a fine drink if taken in the right spirit.
22. Thirst is the end of drinking and sorrow is the end of drunkenness.
23. When the wine is in, the wit is out.
24. When wine sinks words swim.
25. A drunkard's purse is a bottle.
26. Eat at leisure drink by measure.
27. Wine makes old wives wenches.
28. He who drinks a little too much drinks much too much.
29. A good drink makes the old young.
30. There are more old drunkards than old doctors.
31. A cask of wine works more miracles than a church full of saints.

32. Bacchus has drowned more men than Neptune.
33. Take counsel in wine but resolve afterwards in water.
34. "It's not the drinking that is to be blamed, but the excess."
35. Wine makes us princes, love makes us beggars.
36. Wine prepares the heart for love, unless you take too much.
37. There are two reasons for drinking; one is when you are thirsty to cure it; and the other when you are not thirsty to prevent it.
38. The first glass for myself, the second for my friends, the third for good humour and the fourth for mine enemies.
39. Wine to the poet is a winged steed: Those who drink water gain but little speed.
40. And wine can of their wits the wise beguile, make the sage frolic and the serious smile.
41. It has become a common proverb that in wine there is truth.
42. O God, that men should put an enemy in their mouths to steal away their brains.
43. First the man takes a drink, then the drink takes a drink, then the drink takes the man.
44. Drink no longer water, but use a little wine for thy stomach's sake.
45. Wine which music is - music and wine are one.
46. The very best of vineyards is the cellar.
47. Women and wine, game and deceit, make the wealth small and the wants great.
48. Love of a woman and a bottle of wine are sweet for a season, but last for a time.
49. Often have I sought to banish loves pain with wine, but grief turned all the wine to tears.
50. Where there is no wine there is no love.
51. "Most things can be preserved in alcohol. Dignity however, is not one of them."
52. When the drop is inside the sense is outside.
53. Never steal another mans wife and never water another mans whisky.
54. Why should drivellers bore us with the praise of wine
    Whilst we've thee before us wine drink divine.
55. It is better to have bread left over then to run short of wine.
56. The wine of life comes not from battles but from bottles.
57. If wine tells the truth and so have said the wise it makes me laugh to think how brandy lies.
58. Drink for the thirst to come.
59. Pure water is better than bad wine.
60. Wine women and song will get a man wrong.
61. Wine is the discoverer of secrets.
62. Wine fine with a line.

63. Drunkenness and anger, it is said, tell the truth.
64. Wine and youth are like flax upon fire.
65. To serve champagne is to honour those to whom it is served.
66. Drink wine and have the gout, drink none and have it too.
67. Never spare the priest's wine nor the baker's pudding.
68. Beer before wine you'll feel fine: wine before beer you'll feel queer.
69. I'm not so think as you drunk I am.
70. The guests must be chosen as carefully as the wine.
71. Wine is the most healthful and most hygienic of all drinks.
72. Wine is old men's milk.
73. Wine is the best liquid to wash glasses in.
74. Wine is the blood of grapes.
75. Wine not water binds the lovers.
76. Wine makes all sorts of creatures at the table.
77. Thirst is the end of drinking and sorrow is the end of drunkenness.
78. Let's get down on our knees to thank God we're on our feet.

QUOTATIONS

1. "Wine makes daily living easier, less hurried with fewer tensions and more tolerance."
- Benjamin Franklin

2. "Nothing more excellent or valuable than wine was ever granted by the gods to man."
- Plato

3. "A bottle of good wine like a good act shines ever in the retrospect."
- Robert Louis Stevenson

4. "Come, Come, good wine is a good familiar creature if it be well used; exclaim no more against it."
- William Shakespeare

5. "Not only does one drink wine, but one inhales it, one looks at it, one tastes it, one swallows it and one talks to it."
- King Edward VII

6. "By making this wine known, I have given my country as great a service as if I had enabled it to pay back the National Debt."
- Thomas Jefferson

7. "A Californian vineyard has nothing to remind you of the Rhine, The Rhône or the Lower Côte D'or or the infamous and scabby deserts of Champagne; but all is green, solitary covert."
- Robert Louis Stevenson
(The Silverado Squatiers)

8. "Wine is constant proof that God loves us and wants to see us happy." *- Benjamin Franklin*

9. "Drink! For you know whence you came, not why; Drink! For you know not why you go nor where."
- Omar Khayam

10. "Champagne is the only wine that leaves a woman still beautiful after drinking it." - *Madame de Pompadour*

11. "Which famous writer said about drink whetting the appetite but taking away from the performance." - *William Shakespeare*

12. To care for oneself by drinking excellent wine and by eating excellent dishes "that is the proper true education". - *G. Ellwanger 1903*

13. "Somebody left the cork out of my lunch." - *W C Fields*

14. "We drink one another's health and spoil our own." - *Jerome K Jerome*

15. "Wine is only sweet to happy men" - *Keats*

16. "Poetry is devils wine" - *St Augustine*

17. "Wine is the divine juice of September" - *Voltaire*

18. A liking for wine is not a crime and it rarely makes you commit one
Drinkers possess cordiality and openness
They are almost all good. - *Rousseau*

19. Ah! a glass of wine would be very welcome!
Sober my mind is dreamy and silly
I drink a drop
All that is false shatters
Have you noticed that?
Wine sobers you. - *Victor Hugo*

20. He who does not like to drink is very foolish
Because wine fills us with a pleasurable drunkenness
Wine invites us to dance and makes us forget our worries. - *Euripides*

21. Wine lights up the eyes
Warms the mouth
Inflames the body
Illuminates the heart
And makes the mind sparkle. - *Poupon*

22. Old wood is best to burn
Old wine to drink
Old friends to trust
Old authors to read. - *Francis Bacon*

23. Scarcely did I see it (champagne)
When suddenly from my mouth
it entered my heart. - *Abbé de Chateau*

24. Only people wthout imagination
cannot find a good reason
for drinking champagne - *Oscar Wilde*

TOASTS

1. Here's to us who are here, to you that are there, and the rest of us everywhere.
2. Here's to the girl who lives on the hill. What she won't do, her sister will. Here's to her sister.
3. May we love more than yesterday but less than tomorrow.
4. I've known many, liked a few, loved but one - here's to you!
5. Eat, drink and be merry - for tomorrow we diet.
6. May all your troubles be little ones.
7. Until we meet again.
8. Here's to a wet night and a dry morning.
9. Here's to the light heart and the heavy hand.
10. Here's to absent friends and here's twice to absent enemies.
11. May we have a clean shirt and a clean conscience and a bob in the pocket.
12. Thirst is a shameless disease so here's to a shameless cure.
13. May you be in heaven half an hour before the devil knows you're dead.
14. May the wind be always at your back.
15. May we meet again this time next year.
16.

Good Health - Cheers	UK
Slainthe - As above	Ireland
Sante	France
Salute or Cin Cin	Italy
Nazdorovya	Poland - Russia (E Europe)
Prosit	Germany
Salud	Spain
Skol	Scandinavian Countries
Stin Iyia Sas	Greece
Jayawena	India
Ala Sahatik	North Africa
Serefa	Iran
Mabuhay	Philippines
Selamat	Indonesia
Syabas	Malaysia
Swadee	Thailand
Can Chem	Vietnam
Kanpai	Japan
Serefe	Turkey
Lechain	Israel
Dubsida	Korea
Prosit	Austria
Iechyd Da	Wales
Yum Sing	China

17. Here's the health of the salmon to you
    A long life
    A strong heart
    and a wet mouth.
18. May the roof above us never fall in, and may we friends gathered below never fall out.
19. May you live to be a hundred years - with one extra year to repent.
20. May you live as long as you want and never want as long as you live.
21. May you die in bed at 95 years - shot by a jealous wife (or husband).
22. Here's to goodbyes - that they never be spoken!
    Here's to friendships - that they never be broken.
23. May your troubles last only as long as your New Year's resolutions.
24. May you succeed in all you do, long life to you till then.
25. May the best of your past be the worst of your future.
26. Here's to wives and sweethearts - may they never meet.
27. I wish you health - a little wealth, and a happy home with freedom
    And may you always have true friends but never have caused to need them.
28. Drink to me only with thine eyes and I will pledge with mine
    Or leave a kiss within the cup and I'll not look for wine
29. May you get what you deserve and deserve what you get.
30. Arriba, abago, elcentro, eldentro
    Up, down, in the middle, inside (Spanish group toast)
31. May you sail in the sea of ambition and land on the shore of success.
32. May your hand be stretched out in friendship and never in want.

BRAIN TEASERS

1 USING THE ABOVE CIPHER DECODE THE FOLLOWING:

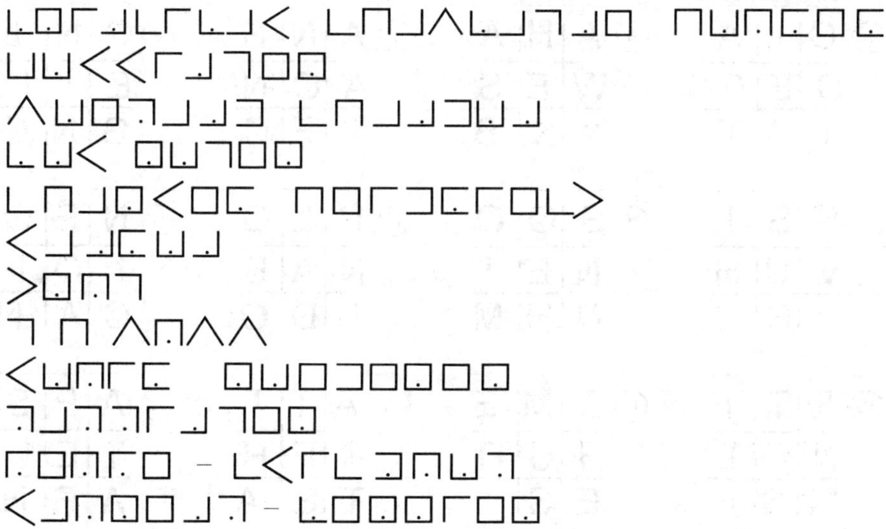

A
B
C
D
E
F
G
H
I
J
K
L

2 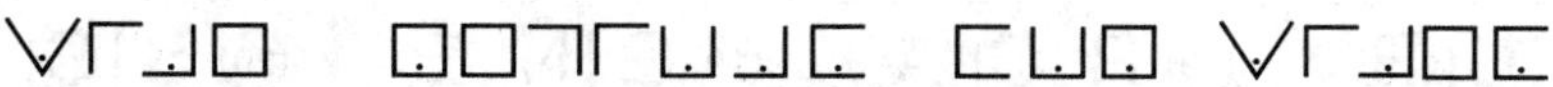

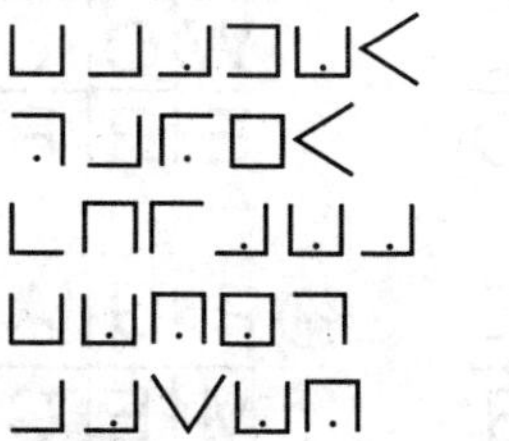

A
B
C
D
E
F

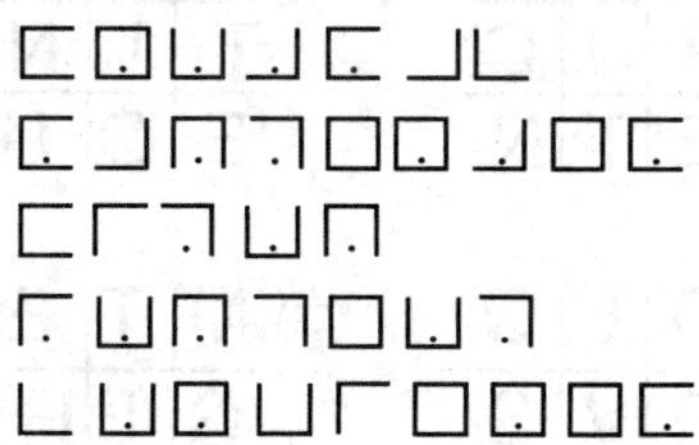

G
H
I
J
K
L

DRINKS TEASERS

Each of the following groups of jumbled letters form a word relating to drink.
To help you on your way the first unjumbled word is MEURSAULT.

(1)
L R S
U A T
U E M
MEURSAULT

(2)
N V E
L I G
E T L

(3)
R M S
C O U
A L B

(4)
T R I
N A H
U B O

(5)
O L A
D E G
I A T

(6)
A H A
W E S
Y K B

(7)
A N R
A O N
I F C

(8)
O N L
E I K
G N O

(9)
S S L
M U H
I B L

(10)
S O O
N E I
N H M

(11)
R L O
N A B
I D O

(12)
N E G
I O T
C A N

(13)
E T I
N O L
M S I

(14)
D M E
H U R
E S I

(15)
A T T
R E R
T S A

(16)
A P S
T E L
A R H

(17)
E C B
R U O
E T N

(18)
R C A
T I N
E O U

(19)
G N E
V A L
C D O

(20)
S C K
W O C
E R R

(21)
D L O
R V S
I C O

(22)
M T E
G I H
A R E

(23)
T N E
R A S
E S U

(24)
P G A
M E C
N H A

25

U	S	C
V	O	L
E	E	C

26

T	C	E
T	I	O
O	R	E

27

U	I	O
B	E	L
U	G	R

28

R	I	F
D	E	F
O	T	I

29

L	I	A
A	U	R
T	S	A

30

V	I	G
O	N	S
N	A	U

31

A	N	C
N	E	S
O	L	E

32

I	T	Z
S	L	I
V	O	V

FIND THE WINE AND EXTRA LETTER HIDDEN IN EACH JUMBLED TRIANGLE BELOW. RE-ARRANGE THE EXTRA LETTER FROM EACH TRIANGLE TO FORM A WINE

LETTER ____

M
A P
E B C
G H N A

WINE ____________

LETTER ____

A
A E
L F N
Z D N I

WINE ____________

LETTER ____

E
A L
E L E
V D L F

WINE ____________

LETTER ____

M
E I
O N T
R M R A

WINE ____________

LETTER ____

O
N N
I I R
O T R P

WINE ____________

LETTER ____

T
I O
L E O
N I S M

WINE ____________

ADDITIONAL WINE ____________

LETTER ____

T
O U
M H B
I N A R

WINE ____________

LETTER ____

E
U U
T A R
A L M S

WINE ____________

LETTER ____

O
R U
E O N
G G B L

WINE ____________

LETTER ______

C
A A
WINE O M N
E S R O

______

LETTER ______

N
P P
WINE R K G
E L I E

______

LETTER ______

I
N T
WINE G N A
Y U Q I

______

ADDITIONAL WINE ______

LETTER ______

M
R A
WINE O C U
C S L B

______

LETTER ______

T
E T
WINE E H S
E P S N

______

LETTER ______

S
S S
WINE N A L
H A E C

______

LETTER ______

V
I S
WINE O C U
C S L B

______

LETTER ______

O
I D
WINE N B L
R O O A

______

LETTER ______

R
A G
WINE N A O
I T A R

______

ADDITIONAL WINE ______

LETTER ______

C
N N
WINE E T B
U R E O

______

LETTER ______

O
N I
WINE A D R
B O O L

______

LETTER ______

O
I N
WINE H R B
U A R T

______

LETTER ______

U
U R
WINE I O B
L E O G

______

LETTER ______

H
A M
WINE P A M
E C N G

______

LETTER ______

A
G G
WINE R E M
E T H I

______

ADDITIONAL WINE ______

LETTER ______

T
G N
WINE A C A
E R H U

______

LETTER ______

T
N O
WINE U S O
A M I L

______

LETTER ______

R
I S
WINE B O E
E C R B

______

LETTER ____

C
T I
WINE S R E
E O S C

____

LETTER ____

D
O A
WINE N A U
G C L E

____

LETTER ____

S
E N
WINE G S E
R B I T

____

ADDITIONAL WINE ____

LETTER ____

L
R N
WINE E M V
L T A O

____

LETTER ____

O
O E
WINE S I A
R B U G

____

LETTER ____

H
L N
WINE N O I
A C L T

____

LETTER ____

T
L O
WINE E I H
E N M D

____

LETTER ____

I
R O
WINE G B U
Y E U L

____

LETTER ____

A
N V
WINE S L C
L E I E

____

ADDITIONAL WINE ____

CROSSWORD 1

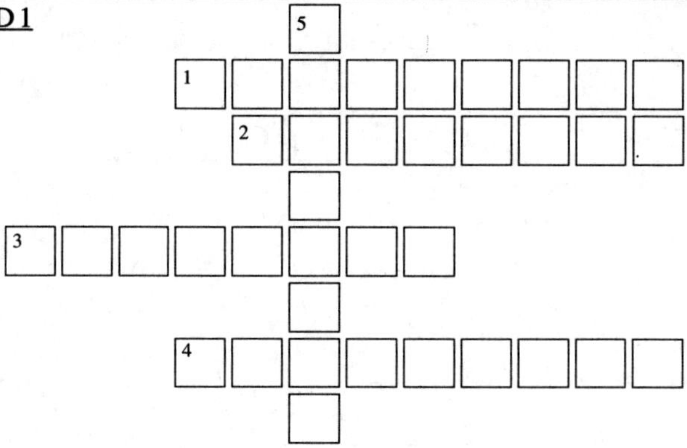

1. Tours will help you find this.
2. Popular with the musketeers.
3. Lady who helped with this riddle.
4. A favourite river tourist stop.
5. A wine region in Eastern France.

CROSSWORD 2

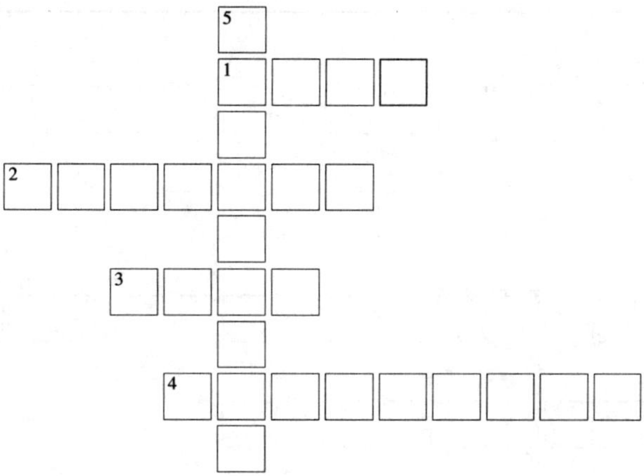

1. Known in Puerto Rico as Tres Castillos.
2. Hang on to your hat.
3. Founded by Johann-Josef.
4. Made from yellow plums.
5. Wines made from Cabernet Franc.

CROSSWORD 3

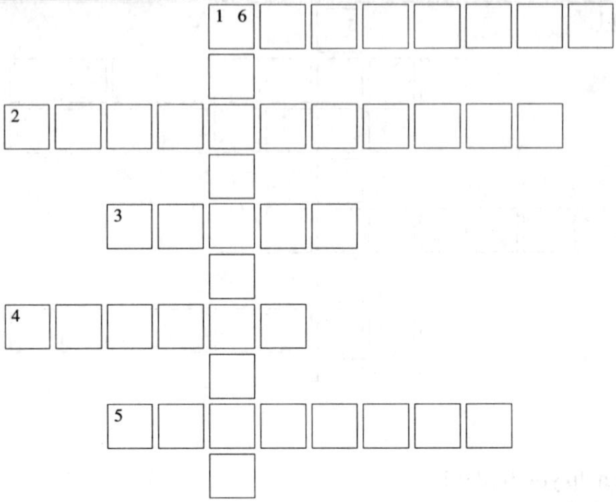

1. White wine from Burgundy.
2. Wine region on west bank of river.
3. A small fruit.
4. Swiss wine region.
5. Named after Italian war hero.
6. This wine has a salty tang to it.

CROSSWORD 4

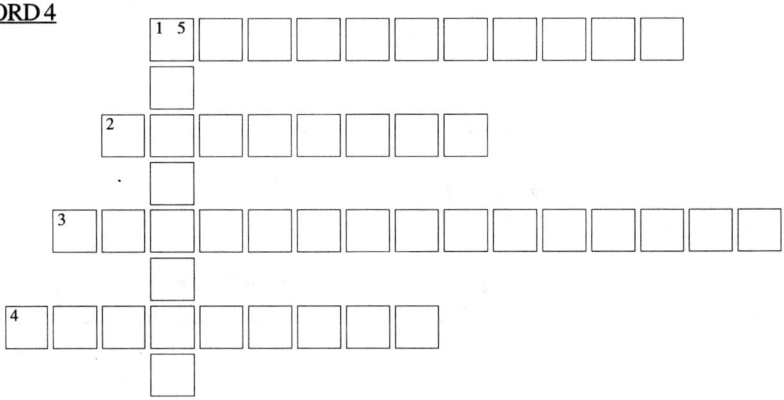

1. To God, most good, most great.
2. Italian wine.
3. Once known as "cuffs and buttons".
4. Home is South Africa.
5. Fixin is made in this region.

CROSSWORD 5

1. Grape once banned by Philippe the Bold in 1395.
2. Blackened roofs caused by manufacture of this drink.
3. Wine region near the Alps.
4. Longest river in this country.
5. Two types Cordon Rouge and Cordon Jaune.
6. A fortified wine.

CROSSWORD 6

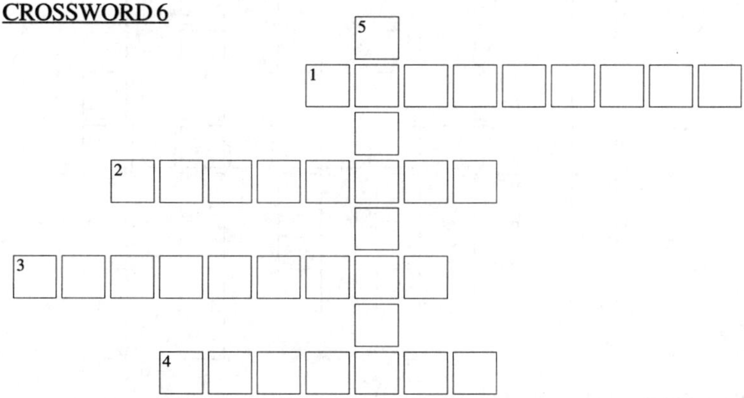

1. Most famous island in the world.
2. A coloured lady.
3. There's a sty in it.
4. Popular liqueur.
5. A nice place to be.

CROSSWORD 7

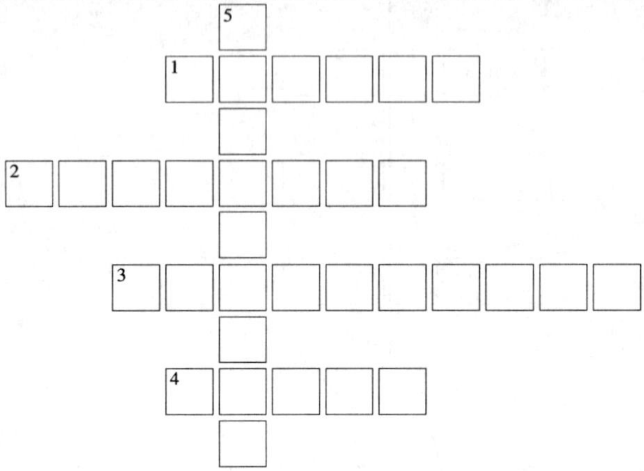

1. Made from the nebbiolo grape.
2. Famous in Bordeaux region.
3. Found in Don Quixote country.
4. Once the drink of the nobility of the region.
5. A national emblem.

CROSSWORD 8

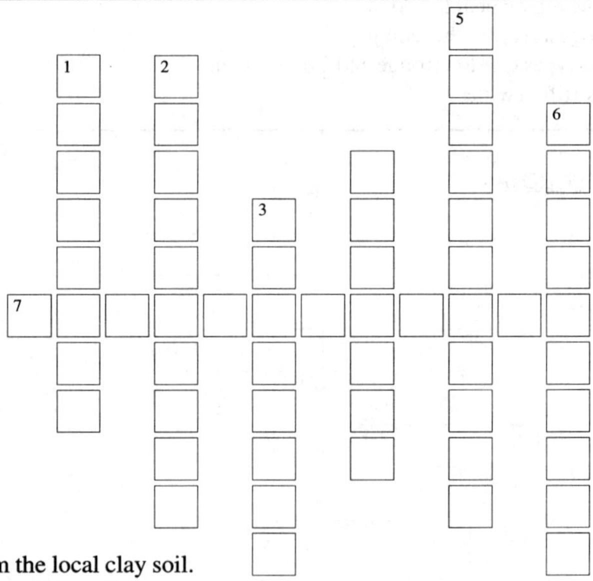

1. Derives its name from the local clay soil.
2. Its name means “valley of stones”.
3. Dolly Parton sings its praises.
4. Driest and lightest in colour of this drink.
5. Add a do to this drink.
6. Goes well with the local olives.
7. A red wine from Italy.

CROSSWORD 9

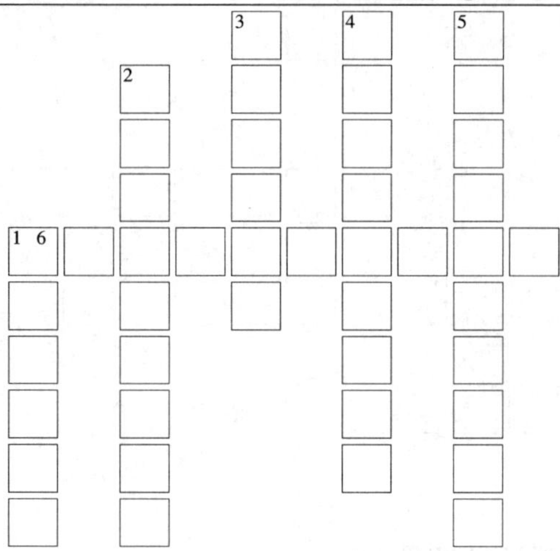

1. A speciality of the Burgundy region.
2. A white plummy drink.
3. Famous writers.
4. Home is South Africa.
5. Named after the dark marasca.
6. Two types available : Green or Yellow.

CROSSWORD 10

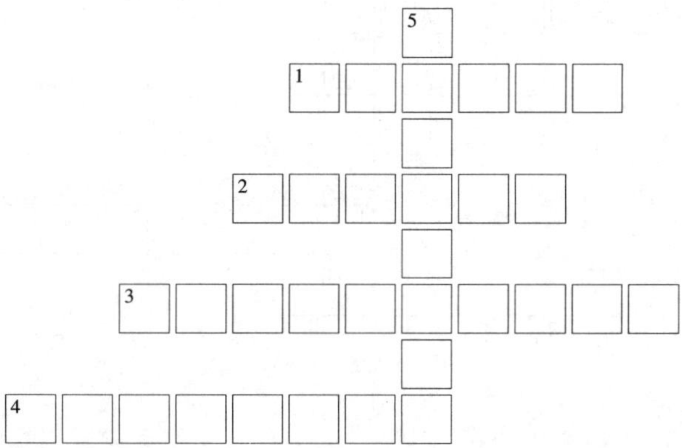

1. Uses unusual form of transport.
2. —ON—
3. This liqueur can be dark red or clear.
4. Wine region.
5. There is an ache in this word.

What do you know about drink?

CROSSWORD 11

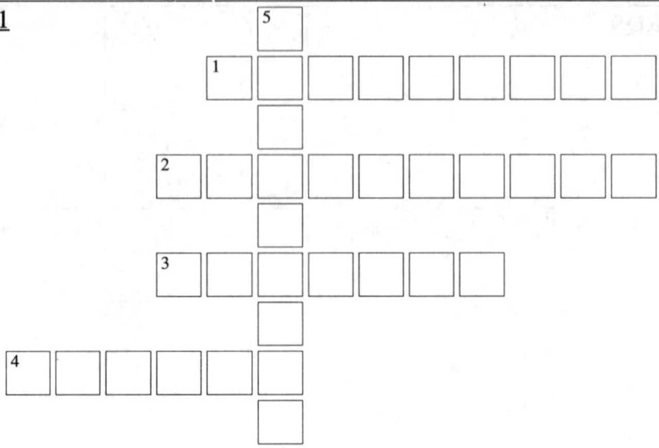

1. Difficult to see in.
2. Reputedly the oldest vineyard in Australia.
3. An island gave its name.
4. Popular tourist destination.
5. Family name given to this drink from Angers.

CROSSWORD 12

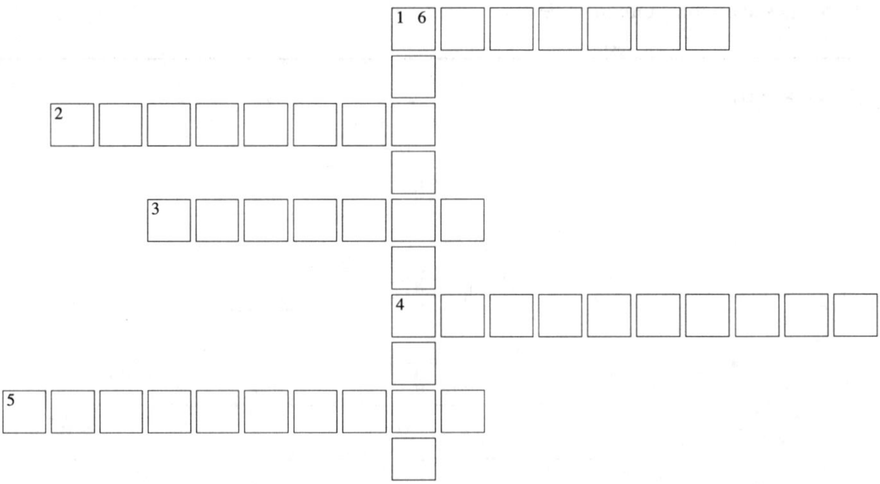

1. Possibly the best known of all Italian red wines.
2. Made with Jamaican run.
3. One of three in Bordeaux.
4. Name means the valley of plenty.
5. A proper one.
6. A grape variety.

CROSSWORD 13

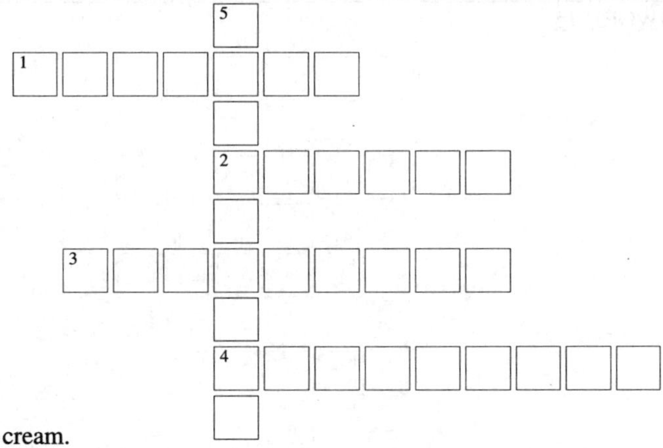

1. Made with fresh cream.
2. Flavoured with a nut.
3. -HI—LAD-
4. Undisputed champions.
5. Some believe St. Patrick planted first grapes here.

CROSSWORD 14

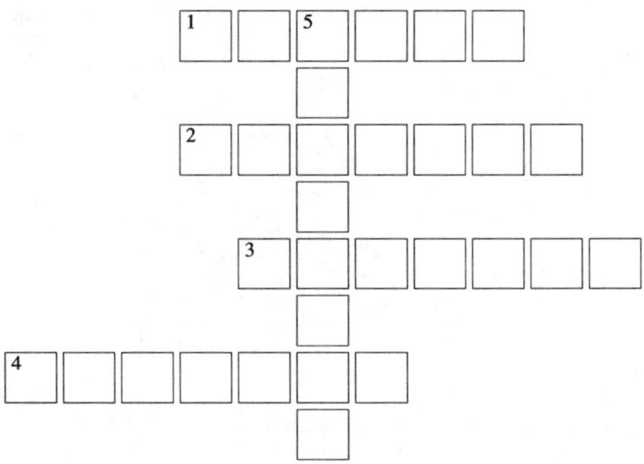

1. West Point is on this river.
2. Two rivers flow into this.
3. LOSE ELM
4. This river flows through a famous wine city.
5. You will find a family pet in this.

CROSSWORD 15

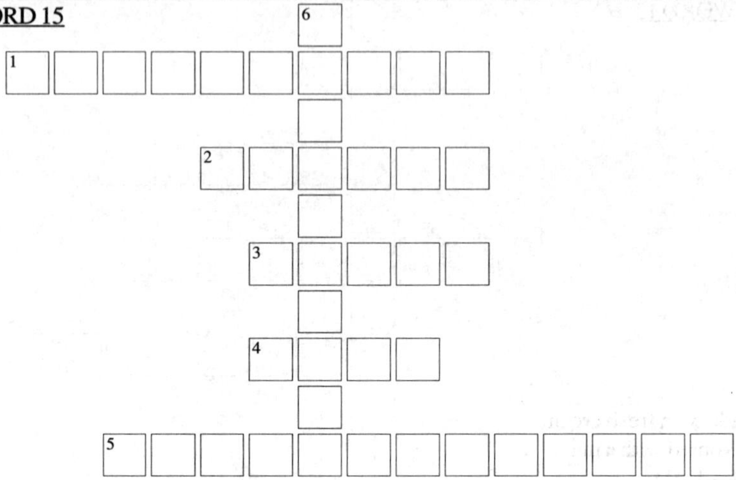

1. Popular liqueur made on the Dalmatian Coast.
2. The vintage for this wine often takes place in mist from which the grape variety gets its name.
3. There is a pear in this word.
4. Greek drink.
5. A town and a grape variety with the same name.
6. Re-use chart.

FRANCE

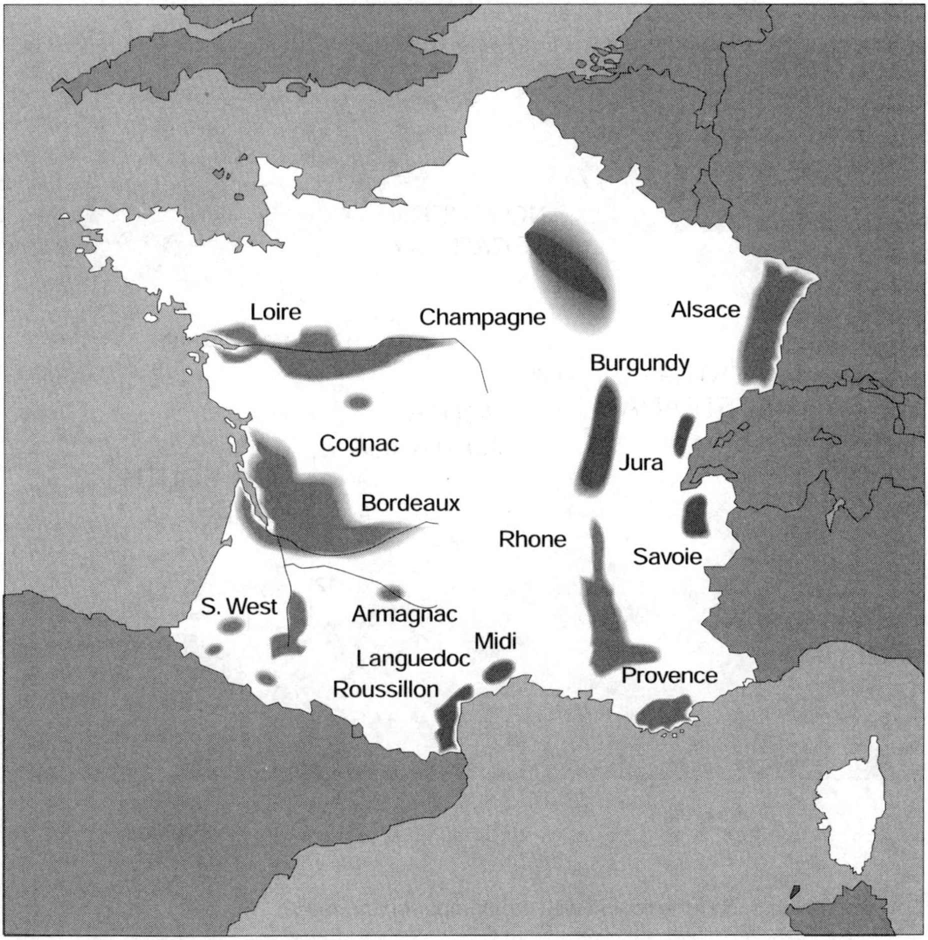

Can you match each wine to its wine growing area:

Arbois
Bandol
Cahors
Fitou
Gewürztraminer
Morey-St-Denis
Sancerre
Seyssel
St Estèphe
St Péray

AUSTRALIA

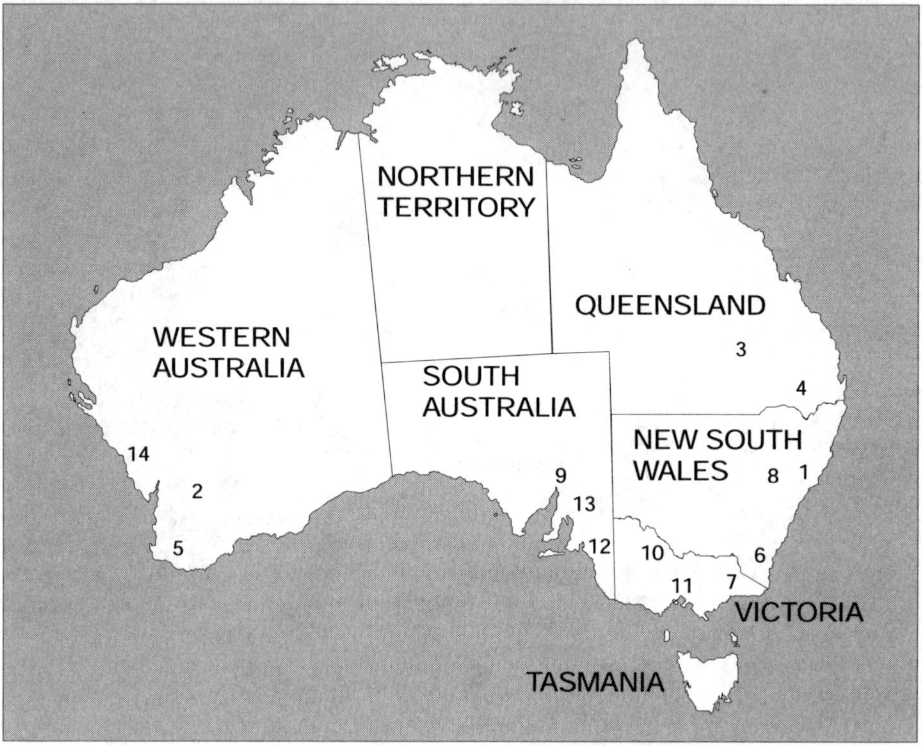

Can you match each wine region with the number on the map?

Barossa Valley
Coonawarra
Geelong
Gin Gin
Goulburn Valley
Hunter Valley
Margaret River
McClaren Vale
Mudgee
Roma
Rutherglen
Stanthorpe
Swan Valley
Yarra Valley

GERMANY

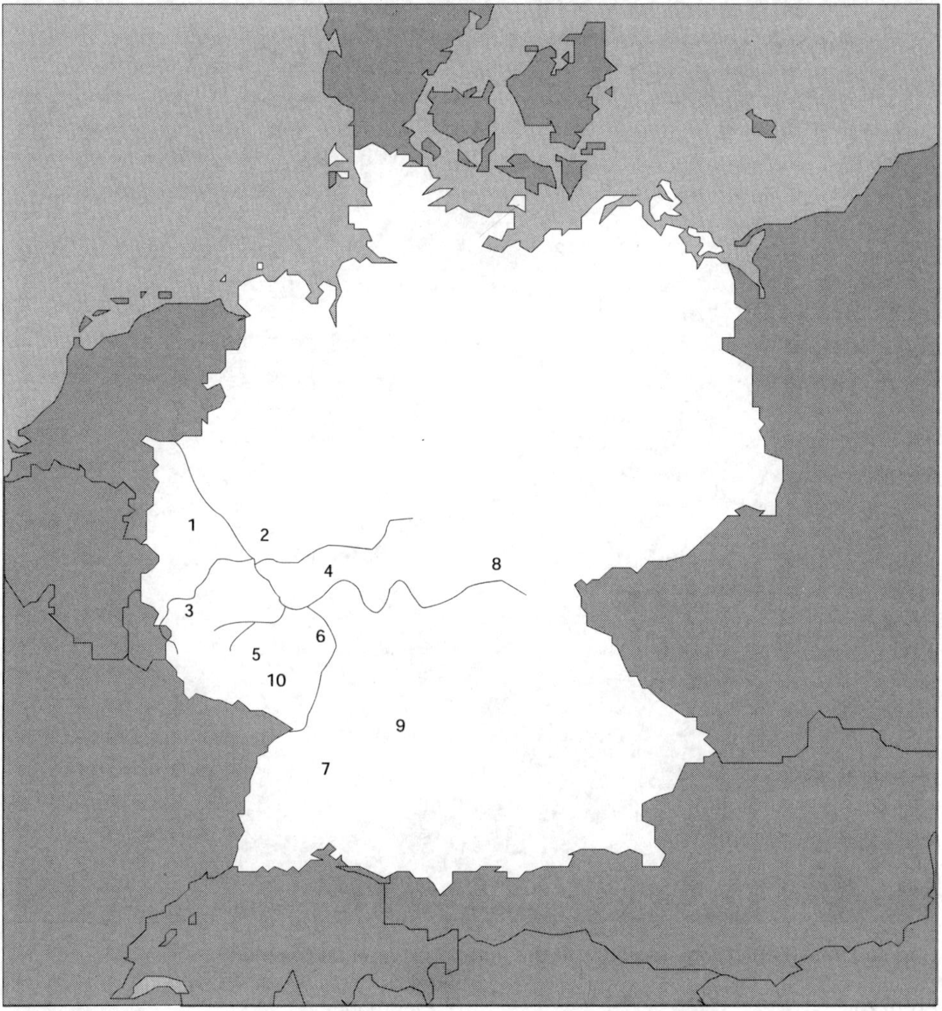

Can you match each wine region with the numbered area on the map

Ahr
Baden
Franken
Mittlerein
Mosel-Saar-Ruwer
Nahe
Reingau
Reinhessen
Reinpfalz
Württemberg

ITALY

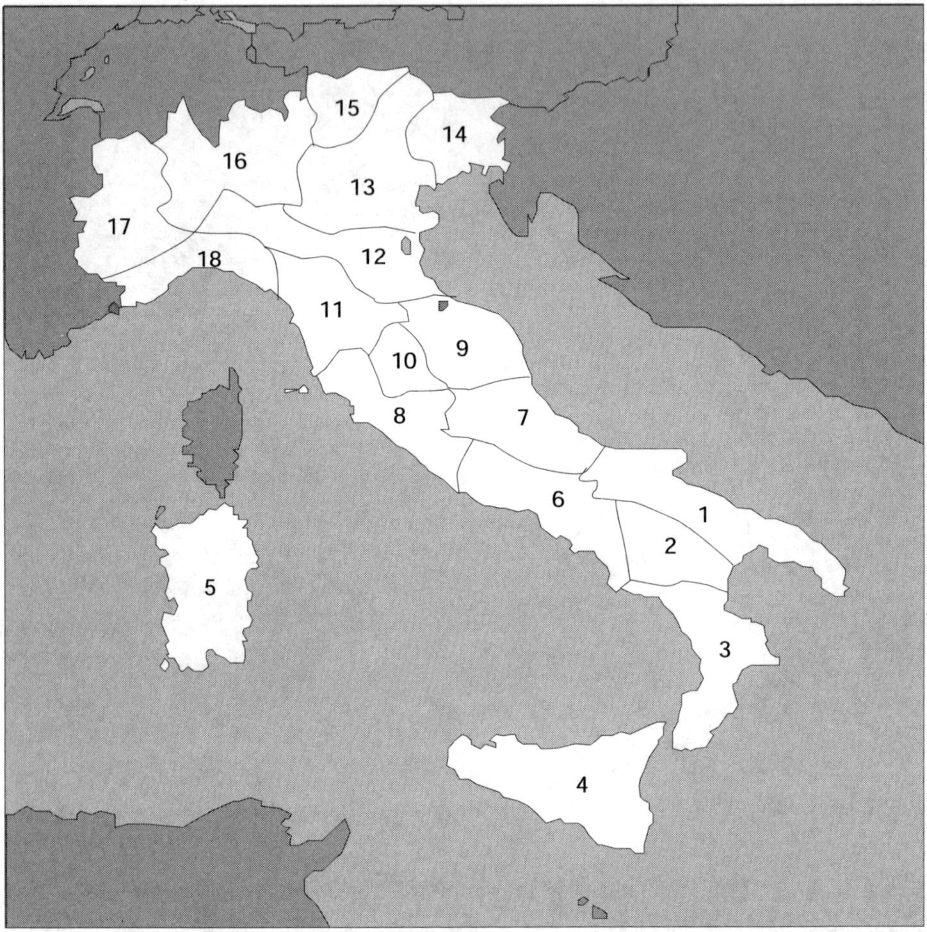

Can you match each wine region with the numbered area on the map?

Abruzzo	Piedmont
Apulia	Sardinia
Basilicata	Sicily
Calabria	The Marches
Campania	Trentino Alto Adige
Emilia-Romagna	Tuscany
Latium	Umbria
Liguria	Veneto
Lombardy	Venezia

NEW ZEALAND

Can you match each wine region with the number on the map?

Aukland
Bay of Plenty
Canterbury
Gisborne
Hamilton
Kumeu
Marlborough
Napier
Nelson
Renwick
Waikanae
Waimauku
Wellington
Whangarei

SPAIN

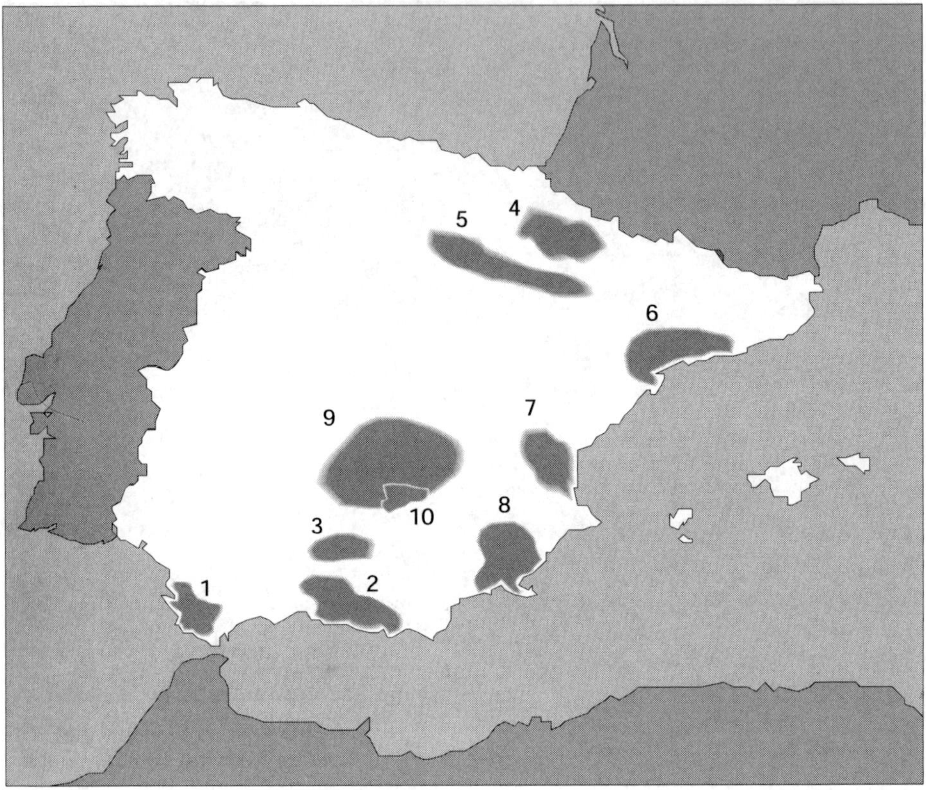

Can you match each wine region with the numbered area on the map

Alicante
Jerez
La Mancha
Malaga
Montilla
Navarra
Penedes
Rioja
Valencia
Valdepenas

UNITED STATES OF AMERICA

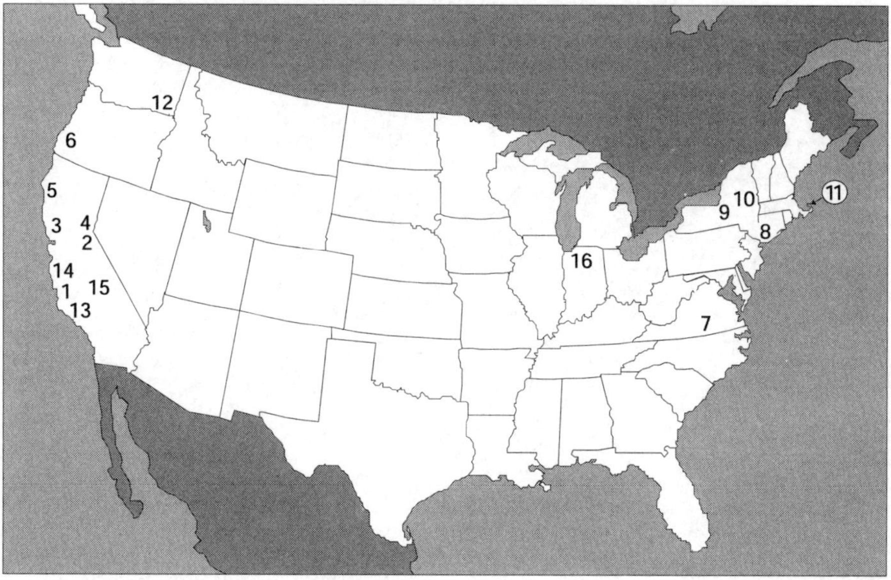

Can you match each wine region with the number on the map?

Dundee Hills
Finger Lakes
Hudson River
Lake Michigan
Long Island
Madera
Martha's Vinyard
Mendocino

Monterey
Monticello
Napa Valley
Santa Barbara County
Santa Clara
Sonoma County
Stags Leap District
Walla Walla Valley

Wordsearch Teasers

CHAMPAGNE

```
V U C O B I R A M V O N T O N I P P U O B I A S O D U C H A R D O N N
P I O O Z J E R O B O W E O R C L A S O D F E R K M E D O A U O B X T
W A U Q C E B E R R M A G R U K R A M N B R P S A R B O U W U O B J F
P Z U C H A M P A G R H Z V S N O D R A H C R G W V U C K O D Y R A C
Y S B R Q C H A M P A U E F R B D R E B E N N Z C H A R D O N N O D O
M A R K U O B O B O N E F R A C K I M E Y U P R A C K I A D O U R E J
G R U N P M A R Q K A U M E R Q M A G J M P R A M J R E B E C Y C H A
G A P M A H C P G A P M A H C D O N T O N I P I A C M A R Q T O N I P
I K C A R R C E B E R S U O B C P I N O T M M S A H E Q I K C A R K C
G A P M A H C N P I N O T M E U N I Y A M J S T A M U H O U O B K B R
V E N R A M O R A M B A U M E R H P I N W E H M A G N S C J T O N I P
E R Q M Z G A P M A H C G R A M G H C Y M A R M E S S A A E H R A H C
E I G A W C H A R D O N N X P I N O O B U E D W E H M A R Y B U U O B
N G K O N B R Z A Y D E U O B Z I O L B Z A U T W U K C H A N E Q H C
G V D B R C U V J O A G R A N D K A E D U A C I P A Q P V U C M R N U
A B V O X C U I S Z D O O C U A G X C H A R D O N N C R M N T O N I P
P I S R J K X A B A U M E R Q E F B O U X D O N O D P E A A D N A R G
M F L E P A G D M A G N R T O N I P U C H A E M A U K G U M U R E M U
A V B J Z E R C U V I R E B E C E H H Y C H A R D O N N I W D S N I P
H C A U F C H A R D O N N Y C U O A P J E R O B O P A S S E L N S A S
C L O N T O N I P W C H A R D R R E B R U R A C K I J R E B E A A G J
R V X A U C C U V Z A U B P W D C N G A M B C H A R D O N N J A C R J
A U I G V D O S A U P I N E O F M C R E I N U E M T O N I P P J E F G
B O R N V R E M U A X D Q N C U A Z G R A N D M A R Q P U O B M V U C
I P L I X N G A M N V H N X T U R B W A S O D G B O U B L B M E S S A
S A K K Z B O R E J N A X B O U U G A P M A H C H C U V O O R D F V O
E J E C J M A R B H Y K C H A R D O N N T C U V G R E M U G O V R A C
D O O A W A U L R A M P F V E G A U M E R K R A M P P I Z U D R A C K
D O E R M R B C B O U X M A R S A S S E M B L A Y H C V X V B O R E J
U O B L R I O N T O N I P F R E B E C N O B O R E J D U A U D O F S A
```

ASSEMBLAGE	AUBE	BOUZY	BRUT
CHARDONNAY	CHAMPAGNE	CUVÉE	DOSAGE
DOUX	GRANDMARQUE	JEROBOAM	MAGNUM
MARNE	PINOT MEUNIER	PINOT NOIR	RACKING
REBECHE	REMUAGE		

BURGUNDY

```
N E F R A C K I M E Y U P R A C K I S R O U R E J G R U N P M A
R Q K A U M E R Q B E A U J O L A I S M A G J M P R A M J R E B
E I R U E L F A P M A N C P G A L P E A H C D O N T O N I P I A
C M A R Q T O N I P I K U A R B C E S E R S U O N O G R O M T M
M S A H E Q I K C A R K C A A P M A I C N P I E O T J M U N I Y
A M J S T A M U H O U O B H E R T D A I D F V P B K M E N R A M
O R A M B A O M E R H P C N W B H M N G N A C J T A N I P E R Q
M Z G A P M N H C G R A M P A G R H N V N N O D R A H C R G W V
U C K O D Y T A C Y S B R Q C H A M O I U E F D B D E E B E N N
Z C H A R D R N N O D O M A R K U O L O B O N E F S A C K I M E
Y M M O N T A G N Y O U R E J G R U A P M A R Q I A U M E R Q M
A G J M P R C M J R E B E C Y C O A H A P M A A C P G A T M A H
C Y O N T O H I P I A C M A R M T O C I P I N C A R R M L H C Y
M A A M E S E A A E G R A H C E I G U W C N A R D O N N U P I N
O O B N E D T E B M I R Y B U U O B N G O O N B R Y A Y A E U O
B Z I O L B Z A U U V U K C H A N E Q L C G V D B R E U S J O A
G R A N D O A E D U R C I P A Q P V A C M R N U A B V R R C U I
S Z D O O C V A G X Y G A R D O N H C R M N T O N I P P U S R J
K X A B A U M E R Q E F U O U X C O N O D P E A R D N A E C M F
B R O U L L Y A G N R T O N I P U C H A E M A U K G U M M R U M
U A V B J Z E R C U V I R E D E C E H H Y C L A R D O N N I W M
S N I P H C A U F C H A R D K Y M D P J U L I E N A I S R M E P
E K U F W C A L N Y E F T W L P U M B G Y F O Y U R F N M S E X
Z K S A I A N N O C A M R S D L J N V X F E S Q K J I F B N P K
```

CHALONNAISE
MONTRACHET
BURGUNDY
JULIENAS
CHABLIS
BEAUNE
RULLY

MOULIN A VENT
MACONNAIS
BROUILLY
MERCUREY
FLEURIE
MORGON
GIVRY

BEAUJOLAIS
MEURSAULT
MONTAGNY
POMMARD
VOLNAY
BEAUNE

BORDEAUX

```
M J P F L E P A L K M G I R X W E D J H Y F O L M J H G Y B F C D K
R F D F Y Y E G D M A G N R T O N I P U C H A E M A A K A U A U R E
M U A V B J T E L H F S E F C X N U O S R H B R O R M L M L N O T C
G E S W K U R B G L I T T K H L F K S T A O Q M O N O C L R X R E K
U B Y H P L U G D E A S N N P I R C U E I R E N E C E I H Y C H A R
D O N N I W S S N I P H O G U R D S E M V K N L F G U J H G T H I M
G T L O G D S E E S A U T E R N E S L I K E G F D A R E O P M V C D
G R S R E S E G T E A I I J K V B Z Q L H F R S P I U E R N V B H K
U T D L O J M B G U R O I O T D S E V I H T Y F R D S L I K N B V C
H T F K N L M U O R D G C S E A W W U O H Y N G V E L I X W E I H F
R K Y L O R E M O R W J P M F T B E S N N F J M C R A X P R T N F K
D Z V E Y W Q M B P D X I M Z E A D W J U G T M V L P G G D F E L Z
M P K U G D E A Q K P E B Y F R K D M B L S T J U L I E N V T G L C
R A G X U E H F M B K L A A Z D Q K I P O N G D R F R V C G P R S E
F X A J M B X H O P A W R U J O K M V G D A R L M A H V X Z R O L J
T D W P L M Y V R Y J H B T X C R H K U Y W Q B C N C K O G H K P Y
S P I B R F C E E X W F U M J D E Z G I Y W Q L K O F G I Y U E Y R
E K G O M B U D E A K J P R X Z E W M L H U T G D S R W Q M N I G C
H H K U I S K O L Y F R C G V D Y Q U E M R J G N U E U N T V Y Z U
P D S R E O E M V C D G R S R E S E G D E A I I J K V N Z Q I H F R
E F I G E R N V B H K U T D L O J M B N U R O I X T D S G V C H Y F
T D S L I K N B V A C H T F K N L M U T O D G C U E A W W U O T O N
S U C H A E M A U R G U M U R E H Y N R S E L I A W K I H F D K Y H
E M O T X R W J P M G T B E S K D T O I E P U C G A E M A U K R U M
T R E M U I V B J Z E L H F S E F R X G T O K R R B R O P M L M O N
S T C G E G W K U O C O D E M K H L O K S L A O A M E N O C I R X D
E K U B Y H P L P G D E A S N N F K V D N O T R M O G R V K U D F N
```

SAUTERNES	ST ESTÉPHE	ST ÉMILION
BORDEAUX	PAUILLAC	ST JULIEN
BERGERAC	DORDOGNE	MARGAUX
GIRONDE	GARONNE	POMEROL
PETRUS	GRAVES	D'YQUEM
BLAYE	MEDOC	BOURG

LOIRE

M F L E P R G D M A G N Q T O N I P U C H A E M A U K G U M U R E M
U A V B J Z U R C U V I R U B E C E H H Y C H A R D O N N I W R S N
I P H U Y H V M R D E S N J I G T Y F D R C E E O L M H U J I G F D
M R W S X G T W U Z L P Y U M N O I H N T G D M M L D U Y O W S R M
B U J H D U Y Z T A D O I M L R C S T O N I P U U H A E L A U K G U
M U S E M U A V B J S E L H F S E Y C X N U O K R F B R O P M L M H
N O T C G E S W K P O B G L I T T K H L F K S L A O Y M E N O C I R
X R E K A B Y H P O P G D E A S N N T O N I P U C H A L M A U K G U
M U R E M D A V B U Z E L H F S E F C X N U O K R H B R L P M T M H
N O T C G E E W K I O B G L I T T K H L F K S L A O Q M E I O C I R
X R E K U B Y T P L P G D E A S N N E J G K M G B F V S O U U I U N
G Y D R G T C S Z L C S E P L U M B J H U G Y R D K M V R H F O Y C
E X R K L S Z T E Y P K M B H T G R S E W J L K O G B A R V T U P Y
X L K P R D W N O S M Y J G H Y T D W S E V X J M P I U J Y F V T I
E X S F G E W K P U N B U G Y C B O U R G U E I L N I P H M B T F E
C W Z J Y B T M L R U J F R I U N T G Y N Y V T E T J U G N T B U G
O Y H G L M U B T L R W M A Y F P B T Y F Y Y H R D E L H F V R U B
N L P I F T W K B O E D W B N I T S X U L M I H Y T C D K U N T Y A
R W M V J G I Y H I E W B K P J R S R L B H F L U M N Y H B R F D E
A K V T C R V R H R S G N G Y D O J I F R H R F H R F B R H U J F R
H F O G T O N I P E I H A E M A U U G U M U R V M U A V B J E E L H
F S E F C X N U O K U H B R O P E L M H N O T C O E S W K U R B G L
I T T N O N I H C L O O Q M E R O C I R X R E K U U Y H P L R G D E
A S N N R E S M J V L T V Y T L G J N T V F G F H P V I R G E E S Z
G U T E I M B L O J T D R W J P O M K H Y D E S T Q J R U M C T V R
X E D F H W K B T V N B F R G P T O N I P U C H A E M A A K N U M U
R E M U A V B J Z E O H F S E F C X N U O K R H B R O P M Y A H N O
T C G E S W K U O B M L I T T K H L F K S L A O Q M E N O C S R X H

POUILLY SUR LOIRE
BOURGUEIL
SANCERRE
QUINCY
LOIRE

POUILLY FUMÉ
MUSCADET
REUILLY
CHINON
ANJOU

MONTLOUIS
TOURAINE
VOUVRAY
SAUMUR

RHONE

```
M L E P P C D M Q A G N T R T O N I E P S C H F A E M A U F H K G N
M U R E X O U B G T D L K M U H N F R T S D C O I U R E M H L J U G
J D H T H T F E S W X R C W C R N Y P M I B U V Y C R X K R Z R W C
E V Y V R E G B Y M K O P U F O Y E O I U Y H U M U K N U E B T M U
C E Z W C B A F R S B U Y R M O R B Y N P L Y H I J U T F E J Y L P
J I M G U L E F S R T U B C G A W N K O L H Y D R M N I T Y F V E C
W X P K I O Y F I Y J B N L Y P T D A F T A V E L T F O S X K I N O
P M Y G B N T R C E S X Q O P K Y N J S K I M B H Y C J N M I T B R
B Y G V H D O F I M V J K O L I P K C U Y T R D R L N F T E W X F R
D S Q J O E N T Y R C E D F Y U P O L A T D C S G S L P D K W P R O
T C M K O U O F E W K H F V E D C L O K R J Y H P K M Y P N E J R E
F R L H G R H T F R B E A U M E D E V E N I S E V D E C W P X K I J
R F G Y E T J I K N M H B T U T G V E D C W L X T R U M A H Y G T M
K J Y T R R E N V V P L O M E T E D W C G F T I R W S P L P M K U Y
T F O T J E M D O G P C O E I A Y I J U E D N H F T U Y H T D F L U
J C T F R T O I I P U C H A R M U U K G U M U R E D U A V B J Z E L
H F S E F C X N T O K R H B D O P G L M H N O T N G E S W K U O H G
L I T T K H L F K A L A O Q N E N O R I R X R E K U B Y H P L P P D
E A S N N W S X J I G N R F O H L O D I T S T Q L K M N Y J M I E Y
R E W S X D C F V G B E N J C K O J I G L A F R D E S W A Q L P S J
N S A D N O G I G X A Z Z S X D C F V E H L B T N Y M U P U M H O Y
T R G V R G V R G J I L K U M H B T V C N Y E R M E M U G T E C J B
U R E I M J N Y E C W Z M K I F W V T G N U G T R E W L M I N Y T A
V B J Z E R C U V I R E B E C E H H Y C H A R D O N N I W D S N S P
```

BEAUME DE VENISE
CÔTE BLONDE
CÔTE BRUNE
ST JOSEPH
LIRAC
CHÂTEAU GRILLET
CÔTE ROTIE
GIGONDAS
ST PÉRAY
TAVEL
HERMITAGE
CONDRIEU
CORNAS

GERMANY

```
M L E P P G D F Q A G N T R T O S S O L H C S F A E M A U F H K G U R
U R E X I U B G R D L K M U H N F R T S D C O I U R E M H L J K G E D
H T H R F E S W X A C W B R N Y O M I B U V Y C R X   R Z E W C I V Y
V R V G B Y M K O P N F T Y G O I U Y H U M U K N U E B T M U N E Z W
C E A F R S B U Y R M C J B Y N P L Y H I J E T F R J Y L P P I M G U
V E F S R T U B N G T W O K O L H Y D R M H I H Y F V E C F X P K I M
Y F I Y J B N L K I T D R N W R U B V T A R S X K M N O A M Y G B H T
R C E S X Q O P K Y E J L K I M B H Y N J N M I T O R L Y U V H I O F
R H E I N G A U P K I W Y E R A R L N F T E W X F S Z Y N R S V H L O
D V T S W Q L K M N Y Y S M I G L U M N H Y B A D E N Y G R D L N V V
P L O M J T E D W C G L T I R W S X L P M K U Y T L R T J E L D E G P
C O E F V Y I S U E I N H F E B Y H T D F L U J B T F R W S X J I S N
E F V H L O P V T N W Q L K M N X B U M J N Y R D H R W H O I M H B E
L B K I G A E Y G M N H Y G T M K J Y G R D E N V V P L O M J T E D A
U G F T T R W S X L P M K R Y T F R T J E L D O G P C O E F V Y I J H
A D N L F T B Y H T D F L O J B T F R W S X J I Y N R R D S N J O I R
F Y E C E D F Y U P O L N T D C S G S L P R H E I N H E S S E N D K W
L S O T C M K K U R F E W W J F V E D C L O K I J Y H P K M K P N U J
E E F R L T G N A T F R V E E C W S X K I J R F G Y H T J I C N M H B
D V T G V E D C W B X T R I M N H Y G T M K J Y G R D E N V O P L O M
E T E D W C G F T I I W S N L P G K U Y T F R T J E L D O G R C O E F
V Y I J U E D N H F T N Y H T I F L U J B T F R W S X J I Y T R F V H
L O D V T S W Q L K M N E J Z I U Y R E W S T K E S V G B H N J M K O
J I G U T F R D E S W A Q T P M J N H B G V F C D S M A Z Z S X D C F
V E V R B T N Y M U P U I H T Y T R G V R G V R G J I R K U M H B T V
R N Y C R M E M U G T R C F B U R E I M J N Y E C W Z M O I F W V T G
N U G Y R E W L M I P Y V A V B J Z E R C U V I R E B E C W H H Y C H
A R D O N N I W D S N D P L F G I K G U N F P C W V R P L J G F S G M
```

RHEINHESSEN	RHEINPFALZ	EDELFAULE
FRANCONIA	KABINETT	RHEINGAU
RIESLING	SPRITZIG	SPATLESE
ROTWEIN	EISWEIN	AUSLESE
TROCKEN	SCHLOSS	BADEN
WORMS	MOSEL	NAHE
SEKT	AHR	

SPAIN/PORTUGAL

U M N H Y G T M K J Y G R D E N V V P L O A D A N A W C G F T I R W
S X A P M K U Y T F R T J E L D O G P C O E F V R I J U E D N H R T
B Y H R D F L U J B T J E L D O G P C O E F V E I J U E D N H A T B
Y H T D S L U J B T F R W S X J I Y N R F V L L O D V T S W Y L K M
N Y Y F M A G L U M N H Y G T M K J Y G R O E N V V P L R A Y T F R
T J E L D O L P C O E F V Y I J U E D N S F T B Y H T D F L U J B T
F R W S X J I A N R F V H L O D V T S W Q H K M N Y U M N O M J T E
D W C G F T I R W S X L P T M U Y T F R T J E L D O G P C O E F V Y
I J U E D N H F T B Y H T D A L U J B T F R W R X J I Y N R F V H L
O D V T S W Q L K M N X B U D W N Y R D H R W H R I M H A G A L A M
G X E Y U M N H Y G T M F R E S N J I Y N R F V H Y O D V T S W Q L
K M N Y U M N H Y G T M K J I G R Y E N V V P L S M J T E D W C G F
T I R W S R M N P T I E B T R C R W S L O H B A P Y M R N W C U J Y
V X L P M K U Y T F R T J E A D O G P C O E T V Y I J U E D N H F T
B Y H T D A L U J B T F R W S X J I Y N R N V H L O D V T S W Q L K
M N Y U M N N Y G T M K J Y G R D E N V I P L O M J T E D W C G F T
I R W S X L P Z K U Y T F R T K J Y G U D E N V V P L O M J T E D W
C G F T I R W S A L P M K H Y G T M Q J Y G R D E N V V P L O M J T
E D W C G F T I R W S X L P M K U Y T F R T J E L D O G P C O E F T
Y I J U E D N H F T B Y H T A F L U J B T S R W S X J I Y N R F V R
L O D V T S W Q L K M N Y R M N M K U Y T E R T F L O R O G P C O O
F V Y I J U E D N H F T B Y H T D F L U J R T F R W S X J I Y N R P
V H L O D V T S W Q L D M N Y P H R S E W C V D E N V V P L O M J T
E D W C G F T I R W A R M N P T I E B T D I H Y G T M K J Y G R D E
N V V P L O M J T I D W C G F T I R W S X A P R W S L O H B D P Y M
R N W C U J Y V R L P M K U Y T F R T J E L D O G P C O E F V Y I J
U O D N H F T C Y H T D F L U J B T F R W S X J P A L O M I N O O D
V L S W Q L K M N Y U M N H Y G T M K J Y G R D E A V V P L O M J T
E O W C G F T I R W S X L P M K U Y A F U T S E L D G G P C O E F V
Y R J U E D N H F T B Y H T D F L U J B T F R W S X J E Y N R F V H
L O D V T S W Q L K M N Y Y F M I G L U M N H Y G T M K D Y G R D E
N S V P L O M J T E D W C G F T I R W S X L P M K U Y T F O T J E L
D O G P C O E F V Y I J U E D N H F T B Y H T D F L U J B T B R W Y

MANZANILLA
QUINTAS
MADEIRA
MALAGA
BODEGA
FLOR

PALOMINO
OLOROSO
MARSALA
SOLERA
TAWNY
PORT

CRIADERA
SERCIAL
ESTUFA
SHERRY
ANADA
RAYA

ITALY

U M N H Y G T M K J Y G R D E S V V P L O M J T E D W P G F T
I A W S X L P M O N I L O D R A B L D O G P I T N A I H C J U
E R N H F T B Y H T D F L U J S T F R W S X J I Y E R F V H L
O S V T S W Q L K M N Y U M N S Y G T M K J Y G M D E N V V P
L A M J T E D W C G F T I R W I X L P M K U Y O F R T J E L D
O L P C O E F V Y I J U E D N C F T B Y H T N F R U J B T F R
B A R O L O N R F V H L O D V A S W Q L V T N Y W V P W U Q J
M O Q U M V U F R E I S A N H I G T M K E Y G R D E I V V P L
O M J T E D W C G S T I O W S A L P M K N Y T F R T J E L D O
G P C O E F V Y I T U E D A H F T B Y H A D F L U J B T T R W
S X J I Y N R F V E L O D V V S W Q L K C N Y V S E M P O O U
Y B H Y N T V R V S K D L U Y E M N H Y C T M K J Y G R D E N
V V P L O M J T E T W C G A T I R W S X I P M K U Y T F I T J
E L D O G P C O E E V Y L J M E D N H F A O Y H T D F T U O B
O F R W S X J I Y S R L V H L B D V T S W Q C C K M A Y T T B
F I S E W M N L O T E J N R X W R Z J U K U M N S C G T M T J
Y G H D E N V V P C O M J T E D W U G F T I R W S E L P M E U
Y T F C T J E L I O G P C O E F V Y S J U E D A H F R B Y C T
D F L U C B T L R W S X J I Y N R F V C L O R V T S W A L L M
N Y U M N I O G T M K J Y G R D E N V V O F O M J T E D B O G
F T I R W P D L P M K U Y T F R T J E L D O G P C O E F V D I
J U E D L H F R B Y H T D F L U J B T F R W S X J I Y N R F A
H L O A V T S W E L A S T I S P U M A N T E K M N Y V Y T G B
J H V E Z W D E L V N Y G R F D K I J U N T M V U R T R W E C

ASTI SPUMANTE	VALPOLICELLA	VERTDICCHIO
BARBARESCO	LAMBRUSCO	BARDOLINO
EST EST EST	SASSICAIA	VERNACCIA
PIEMONTE	FRASCATI	DOLCETTO
CHIANTI	MARSALA	ORVIETO
FREISA	BAROLO	SOAVE

EUROPE

U M C H Y G T M K J Y G R D E N V V P L O M J T E D W C G F T I R
W S O L P M K U Y T F R T J E L D O G P O B E F V Y I J U E D N H
F T D Y H T D F L U J B T F R W S X J S Y N E F V H L O D V T S W
Q L E M N Y U M T I K V R N H Y G T C K J Y G Y D E N V V P L O M
J T M D W C G F T I A I N O L A T A C Y T F R T C E L D O G P C O
E F V Y I J U E D N H F T B Y H T D F L U J B T F H W S X J I Y N
R F V H L O D V T S W Q L K V O E S X M N Y U M N H E G T M K J Y
G S T T U P V P L O M J T E D W C G F M I K W S X L P V K U Y T F
R T J E L D O G P C O C F V Y I J U E D A H F T B Y H T E F L U J
B T F A L B A R I N O O F V H L O D V B S R Q L K M N Y V L Y G M
N H Y G T M K J Y G R N E N V V P L I M J T C D W C G F I I L R S
X L P M K U Y T F R T D E L D O G N C O E F V H I J U E O N H E T
B Y H T D F L U J B T R R W S X E I Y N R F V H E O D V G S W B L
K M N Y U M N H Y G T I K J Y T R D E N V V P L O M J T N D W S G
F T I R W S X L P M K E Y T T R T J E L D O G P C O E F I Y I S U
E D N H T T B Y H T D U L U J B T F R W S X J I Y N R F E H L O D
V T S W Q O E M N Y U M N H Y G T M K J Y G R D E N V V R L O L J
T E D W C G K I I R W S X L P M K U Y T F R C J E L D O G P C H E
F V Y I A U E A R H F T B Y H T D F L U J H T F R W S X J I Y C R
F V H L I D V N Y U R M N U C F R S W C A S W Q L K M N Y U M S H
Y G T M V J Y G R D E N V V P L O M J B E D W C G F T G R W S X L
P M K U A T F R T J E L D O G P C O L F V Y I J U E D N R F M B Y
H T D F D U J B T F R W F X J A N I S T E R L O D V T S W A L K M
N Y U M L H Y G T M K J Y G R D S N V V P L O M J T E D C C V F T
I R W S O L P M K U Y T F R T J E L D O G P C O E F V O I J U E D
N H F T M Y H T D F L U J B T F R W S X J I Y N R F N H L O D V S

BEYCHEVELLE	SCHLOSSBERG	CATALONIA
KABINETT	ALBARINO	VIOGNIER
MOLDAVIA	CONDRIEU	CHABLIS
FLEURIE	MOSCATO	RETSINA
MARCHE	GRAVES	MACON
MEDOC	TOKAY	PUTTS

LIQUEURS

U M N H Y G T M K J Y G R G E N V V P L O M J T E D W C C F T I
R W S X L P M K U Y T F R A J E L D O G P C O E F V Y U J U E D
N H F T B Y H T D F L U J L T F R W S X J I Y N R F R H L O D V
T S W Q L K M N Y D T I R L S X W S X L P G K U Y A F R T J E L
D O G P C O E F V Y I J U I D N H F S X J I L N C F V H L O S V
P Y B T D R E C M N B Y B A S W Q L K M N T I A W S X L P I K U
Y T F R T J E L D O G P C N E F V S I J U E O N Y F T B S H T D
F L U J A T F R W S X J I O N R F V Y L O D V T S V Q S K M N Y
B E N E D I C T I N E G R D E N V V P E O M J T E D A B Y H T D
F L U J V T F R W S X J I Y N R F V H L L D V N U C R M N U C F
R S W C O S W Q L K M N K U M N H Y G T M I J U G R D E N V V P
L O M J C E D W C G F U I R W S X L P M K U A T F R T J E L D O
G P C O A F V Y I J M T D N H F T B Y H T E F B U J B T F R W S
X J I Y A R F V H M O D R T S W Q L K M R Y U M N H Y G T M K J
Y G R D T N V V E L O M J O E D W C G T T I R W S X L A M K U Y
T F R T J E L L O G P C O E F V Y I N U E D N H F T B Y I T D F
L U J B T F R W W C G F T I R M S I L P B K U Y T F R T J H L D
O G P C O E F V Y I J U E D N H O T B Y R T D F L U J B T F A W
S X J I Y N R F V H L O D V N C F C M N O C F R S W C T S W Q B
K M N Y U M N H Y G T M K J Y G R D N N N V P L O M J T E D W C
G F T I K W S X L P M K U Y T F R T J R T D O G P C O E F V Y I
J U E D N A F T B Y H T D F L U J B T F E W S X J I Y N R F V H
L O D V T S H Q L K M N Y U U N H Y G T M H J Y G R D E N V V P
L O M J T E D L C G F T I R B S X L P M K L T M K U Y T F R T J
E L D O G P C O U F V Y I J I E D N H F T B Y U T D F L U J B T
F R W S X J I Y N A F V H L L D V T S W Q L K M O Y U M N H Y G
T M K J Y G R D E N V V P L A M J T E D W C G F T S R U Y T F R
T J E L D O G P C O E F V Y M J U E D N H F T B Y H T D F L U J
B T F R W S X J I R E I N R A M D N A R G B T D R E C M N B Y B

SOUTHERN COMFORT	GRANDMARNIER	BENEDICTINE
COINTREAU	GALLIANO	ADVOCAAT
BAILEYS	CURACAO	KAHLUA
KUMMEL	GLAYVA	MALIBU
BRONTE	CASSIS	BAHIA

COCKTAILS

```
L P M K U Y T F R T J E L D O G P C O E F V Y I J U E B N H
F T B Y H T D F L U J B M A P L E L E A F N R F V H R O D V
H U F R M N U C F R S W C I S W Q L K F N Y U M N O Y G T M
K A Y G R D E N V V P L O Q J T E D I C G F T I N W S X L P
M K R Y T F R T J E L D O U P C O R F V Y I J X E D N H F T
B Y H V D F L U J B T F R I S X S I Y N R F V H L O D V T S
W Q L K E N Y U M N H Y G R M T J R G R D E N V V P L O M J
T E D W G Y F T I R W S X I N M K U E T N N O O M Y E N O H
C O E F V O W J U E D N L I M K U Y T Y R E J E L D P G P C
O E F V Y I F A E D N H G T B Y H T D F A U T B T A R W S X
J I Y N R F V N L O D H T S W Q L K M N Y R M T R Y G T M K
J Y G R D E N V O L T O M J T E D W C G F T P A A F T B Y H
T D F L U J B T F D B S X J I Y N R Y V H L D S V H Y B T D
R E C M N B Y B T S N A L K M N T D R W S I L P N K N Y T F
R T J E L D O G P C O O N V Y I A U E D S H F T B E H A D F
L U J B T F R W S X J I L G R L V H L E D V T S W Q D K M N
Y U M N H Y G T M K J Y G R E E N V V P L L M J T E D I C G
F M I R W S X L P M K U Y T F R T J E L D I G P C O E F A Y
I J A E D N H F T B Y H I D F L Y J B T F A W S X J I Y N M
F V H L O D V N U F R H N U C F D S W C T N W Q L K M N Y U
M N H Y S T M K J Y W R D E N V A P L O M Y T E D W C G F T
I R W S X D P M K U Y T F R T J L L D O G T C O E F V Y I J
U E D N H F N B Y H T D F L U J K T F R W S N Y L K O O R B
H L O D V T S A Q L K M N Y U M N H Y G T U K J Y G R D E N
V V P L O M J T R D W C G F T I I W S X L R M K U Y T F R T
J E L D O G P C O G B T D E M L P K K H I F O C E B I O N T
```

HARVEY WALL BANGER
WHITE LADY
HONEYMOON
MANHATTEN
DAIQUIRI

MAIDENS PRAYER
MAPLE LEAF
GRAND SLAM
PINK LADY
BROOKLYN

FIRST NIGHT
LONDON FOG
RUSTY NAIL
PARADISE
BRONX

MINERAL WATERS

```
L P M K U A T F R T J E L D O G P C O E F V Y B J U E D N H F T M
Y H T D N L U J B T F R W S X J I Y N R F V H U O D V N U F R A N
U C F N S W C T S W Q L K M N Y U M N H Y G T X K J Y G R D L N V
V P A O M J T E D W C G F T I R W S X L P M K T Y T F R T V E L D
O P P S O E F V Y A P P O L I N A R I S I J U O D N H F E B Y H T
D F L U H B T F R W S X J I Y N R F V H L O D N T S W R L K M N Y
U M N H Y B T M K J Y G R D E N V V P L O M J T A D N C G F T I R
W S X L P M O U Y T F R T J E L D O G P C O E F V G I J U E D N H
F T B Y H T D U L U J B T F R W S X J I Y N R F V H O O D V P Y B
T D R E C M N B R B T S W Q L K M N T I R W S X L P M W U Y T F R
T J E L D O G P C N E F V Y I J U E D N H V T B Y H T D Y L U J B
T F R W S X J I Y N E F V H L O D V T S W I L K M N Y U M L H Y G
T M K J Y G R D E N V V P L O M J T E D W T G F T I R W S X L P M
K U Y T F R T J E L O O G P C O C F V Y I T U E D N H F T B Y A T
D F L U J B T F R W L X J I Y N R O V H L E D V N U F R M N U C B
R S W C T S W Q L K V N Y U M N H Y N T M L F Y G R T E N V V P L
O M J T E D W C G F I I R W S X L P M T U A T F R T I E L D O G P
C O E F V Y I J U E C N H F T B Y H T D R L U J B T O R W S X J I
Y N R F V H L O A V T S W Q L K M N Y R M E H Y G T D K J Y G R D
P E R R I E R M J L E D W C G F T I A W S X X P M K A Y T F R T J
E L D O G P C O W S L J I Y N R F R H L O D V N U F B M N U C F R
S W C T S W Q L K M N E U M N H E G T M K J Y G R D E N V V P L O
M J T E D W C G F T I R V S X L P M K U Y T F R T J E L N A I V E
O E F V Y I J U E D N H F T L Y H T D F L U J B T F R W S X J I Y
N R F V H L O D V T S W Q E N M N Y Y M N H Y G T W O R S C J U M
L P E W Q X F R M N B O I T M O J Y G R D E N V V P L O M J T E D
W C G F T I R W S X L P M K U Y F F R T J E L D O G P C O S P A H
```

APPOLLINARIS	FERRARELLE	BALLYGOWAN
ASHBOURNE	FONTVELLA	CONTREX
MALVERN	PERRIER	VOLVIC
VITTEL	BUXTON	BADOIT
EVIAN	PANNA	SPA

Answers

Part 1

GENERAL

1. Over fourteen years if the licence permits them
2. Yes
3. Yes
4. Yes and so can those staying there or passing to other parts of the premises.
5. A licence which allows sales from Monday to Saturday. On Sundays only residents can be served
6. Yes except with a doctor's permission or for an urgent medical case
7. It is an offence for anyone to drive a motor vehicle with more than 80mg of alcohol in every 100ml of blood
8. No
9. Yes
10. Yes
11. Yes
12. Malaga
13. Full bodied
14. Light bodied
15. Dean Martin
16. Jack Lemmon
17. American name for apple brandy
18. A cocktail consisting of vodka, lime juice, ginger beer, ice strained before serving
19. A cocktail consisting of vodka, tomato juice, Worcester sauce, lemon juice, salt, pepper, ice, celery salt
20. A sweet yeast cake cooked with rum syrup
21. Marsala
22. Marsala
23. England (Felstead, Essex)
24. Elvira, Diana, Isabella, Cynthiana, etc.
25. Lebanon
26. Hampshire
27. Cramant is a wine producing village in the Champagne region. Crémant is a French term which literally means creaming and applied to mildly sparkling wines
28. Not more than two thirds full
29. Upright
30. Sommelier
31. A wine which has a predominance of one grape variety and uses the name of that grape for the name of the wine
32. Vin Jaune is a yellow wine produced in the Jura region of France from the sauvignon grape
33. Tocay
34. The most famous red wine of Hungary produced in the Eger district about 120 miles NW of Budapest. The Hungarian name for this wine is EGRI Bikaver which means "Bulls blood from Eger"
35. Noble rot is a fungus or mould that attacks certain grapes in certain regions given favourable conditions.
36. Retsina
37. These drinks are made by layering liqueurs, spirits, syrups in a glass on top of each other depending on the specific gravity of each
38. Loving Cup
39. Isinglass, a geletine substance often obtained from the swim bladder of the sturgeon.
40. A wine which has had a spirit added to it during or after fermentation
41. Cognac is a brandy produced in a legally defined area of SW France and is protected by law
    Only brandies produced in this sharply defined area can be called Cognac. Rated the best brandy in the world.
42. Copita
43. A fee paid to a restaurant for allowing customers to bring in their own wines to be consumed in the restaurant
44. A visual measure which is automatic and gives a pre-set measure
45. Spain
46. A waiter's friend is a small knife with a corkscrew and lever attached for opening bottles.

47. 75cl (26.4 fl. ozs)
48. 750ml
49. 40% alcohol by volume
50. Chianti Classico
51. A pale green tinge
52. Purple
53. England (Kew Gardens)
54. Bacchus
55. Yes. Tedesche Winery produces wine.
56. A term used by a wine taster to describe a wine that makes the mouth pucker which is an indication of excess of tannin.
57. Yes
58. By grafting European wines onto phylloxera resistent roots of native American wine stocks
59. Napa Valley California
60. New Zealand
61. Sonoma County California
62. A cross vine of two grape varieties in an attempt to combine the best qualities of both
63. Kenwood, Beaulieu, Beringer, Inglenook, Sterling, Krug, Christian Brothers, Martine, Mondavi, Stags Leap, Gallo, etc.
64. Sabastiani, Buena Vista, Chateau St Jean, Hanzell, Hacienda, Clos du Bois, Simi, Souverain, etc.
65. Washington, Oregon Ohio, Iowa, Arizona, Connecticut, Georgia, Maryland, Massachusetts, Michigan, Minnesota, Missouri, Carolina, etc..
66. Aniseed flavour
67. Aniseed liquorice flavour
68. The name given to the special vat used in the making of Port
69. Gin gets its name from the French word for juniper (Genievre). First made in Holland in 1577
70. Best from rye but can be made from other grain. Vodka means "little water".
71. Glen Grant, Glenfiddich, Glenlivet, Glenfarcias, Tamdhu, Strathisia, Tamnavulin
72. England (Kent)
73. Bouquet or aroma
74. Vaud
75. Chile
76. South American brandy, 45% alc by vol.
77. Dole
78. Bulgaria
79. Best quality wine
80. Austria
81. Water
82. A wine that has been fully fermented out, less than 2% or no sugar remaining.
83. To bottle wine directly off its lees - the light sediment which is deposited during fermentation without firstly racking
84. Marc (French) Grappa (Italy)
85. Bottled (it can be taken as a mark of added quality)
86. Barrique
87. 6 glasses
88. 14-16 glasses
89. Origin of the wine, appropriate description, name and address of bottler or shipper, volume in litres or centilitres
90. San Joaquin Central Valley California
91. Wine of Kings
92. 5 fl ozs or a quarter of a pint
93. Six measures from a gill
94. Units of alcohol
95. Marlborough, Hawkes Bay, Wairarapa, Canterbury, etc.
96. Hunter Valley, Barossa Valley, Coonawara, Yarra Valley, Clare Valley, Margaret River, Mudgee, etc.
97. Sake
98. Tannin
99. Unfermented grape juice
100. 3 years
101. A red grape variety used in the making of the Portugese wine DAO.
102. Fermentation.
103. To keep the cork moistened by the wine otherwise it will dry out and allow air to penetrate the bottle which will cause spoilage to the wine
104. Yes

105. Grog is a hot toddy usually made with rum and hot water
106. Blindness
107. 100 litres
108. Scotland
109. True
110. Hungary
111. Rhine
112. New Zealand
113. Rhône
114. Winchester (Quart - 40 fl ozs)
115. Yugoslavia
116. A wicker-wrapped bottle
117. Punt
118. It is, It is, It is.
119. Moet et Chandon
120. Brandy
121. Vintage port is an outstanding wine of an outstanding year, then put in casks for 2 years and bottled for 15 years
122. An average of about 3 per decade
123. A method of planting vines in the Rhone region
124. Malt Whiskies
125. Argentina
126. (a) Sight/Appearance, (b) Nose/ Bouquet, (c) Palate/Taste, (d) Summary of overall impression
127. Aeneas Coffey
128. Pinot Noir
129. Chardonnay
130. Sambuca
131. Ethyl alcohol
132. Cognac
133. Smothers Winery Santa Cruz California.
134. To serve wine clear leaving the sediment in the bottom of the bottle
135. Samuel Henshall in 1795
136. Master of Wine
137. Touraine in the middle of the Loire
138. Serve at room temperature (16 degrees C - 20 degrees C)
139. 7 - 10 degrees C
140 7 - 8 degrees C
141. The name given to gin by soldiers of King James the First
142. Aquavit
143. South Australia
144. Near Sydney in 1788
145. Islay, Jura, Skye, Mull, Orkneys
146. A cocktail consisting of whisky, lemon or lime juice, sugar shaken over ice garnished with a slice of orange and a cherry
147. Southern Comfort
148. Douro Region
149. Pauillac, Margaux, St Julien, Moulis, Listrac St Estéphe etc.
150. Côtes de Nuits Gevrey Chambertin Beaune/Chablis Montagny, Rully etc.
151. Sylvaner, Gewurztraminer, Pinot Gris, Pinot Blanc, etc.
152. Bandol, Cassis Bellet Palette/Pradel Rosé Bellet Rosé Bandol Rosé etc.
153. Hermitage, Gigondas Chateauneuf-Du-Pape/Condrieu/St Péray
154. Chinon
155. Asti Spumante, Barbera, Barolo, Freisa, Cortese, etc.
156. Orvieto, Torgiano, Colli Del Trasimeno, etc.
157. Chianti, Galestro, Brunello Di Montalcino, Sassicaia, etc.
158. Verdicchio Dei Castelli, Verdicchio Di Matelica, Rosso Conero, etc.
159. La Cryma Christi Taurasi, Greco Di Tufo, Solopaca, etc.
160. Soave, Valpolicella, Bardolino, Recioto, Amarone Piave, etc.
161. Germany
162. Pears
163. Benedictine (Deo Optimo Maximo means "To God Most Good Most Great"
164. 78 degrees C
165. Champagne
166. False
167. Cana in Galilee
168 2.8 - 3.8 (lower figure is ten times more acidic)
169. Measured as a percentage of volume
170. A standard measure of spirits fortified wine and beer (half pint) contain the same amount of alcohol 10ml; this is referred to as one unit of alcohol

Note: a glass of wine (one sixth of a bottle) contains 1.5 units of alcohol

171. 8 grams is equal to 1 unit of alcohol
172. One hour
173 21 units for a man and 14 units for a woman
174. The elderly, pregnant women and the young are more at risk
175. A treaty signed in 1703 between England and Portugal giving the wines of Portugal preferential taxation over that for French wines.
176. The Franconian wines of Germany are traditionally sold in flat sided type bottles
177. Chile
178. Chile
179. France
180. Luxenbourg
181. 21st
182. Rice
183. Melon
184. Irish Whiskey, cream, chocolate
185. Bananas
186. Martinique
187. Bordeaux
188. Trinidad
189. From the old town of Angustura in Venezuela. The town is now called Ciudad Bolivar
190. French aperitif red wine made from quinne herbs oils etc.
191. A sweet red aperitif wine from Corsica.
192. An aperitif wine (red or white) from Bordeaux
193. A rich sweet wine from the Friuli-Venezia-Giulia region of Italy
194. Holly berries
195. Elderberries
196. Sloes and their kernals.
197. Napa Valley California.
198. Fargues Sauternes Bordeaux.
199. Cerons Bordeaux.
200. Van Gogh
201. Russia
202. Romania
203. Greece
204. U.S.A.
205. Australian Brandy
206. 1 cup of cold tea, 1 raw egg, 1 teaspoon of honey - shake over ice, strain and serve
207. - 117 degrees C.
208. Madeira
209. Greece
210. Gin and ginger beer - this is known as a little dog. Gin and light ale is known as a big dog
211. One part Spanish brandy to three parts fresh orange juice
212. Whiskey/Whisky
213. 40ml or 1.25 fl ozs
214. A South Tyrol grape variety pinot nero called Blauburgunder (Blue Burgundy).
215. Finland, made from culled Cloudberries
216. A glass vessel
217. Mexico
218. The finest Cognac brandy and is a blend of Grande and Petite Champagne Cognacs with a minimum of 50% Grand Champagne
219. Timber
220. Italy
221. Château Grillet
222. 9 litres (12 x 75cl)
223. China
224. Avellino Campania Italy
225. Arrack
226. Between 9 and 15 degrees
227. Between 15 and 22 degrees
228. La Ciguena Navarra
229. Australian Wine Bureau
230. (a) Tip of tongue (b) Front upper sides (c) sides (d) centre and rear
231. Approx 10% - 73 million litres in 1997 - $260 million
232. California
233. At the Bouna Vista winery Sonoma County California
234. Napa Valley
235. Ernest and Julio Gallo, Modesto California.
236. Pradel Rosé
237. 1775

238. Ferruccio Lamborghini makes red and white wine at Lago de Trasimeno
239. Chile
240. A drink into which has been added a drug to make the drinker unconscious.
241. At Irish Distilleries, Midleton, Cork, Ireland
242. 130,625 litres or 30,000 gallons
243. Made into dry white wine - AC Bordeaux Blanc
244. Used for fining
245. From the River Rio OJA
246. 4-7 egg whites to 225 litres approx.
247. Bentonite
248. Nicolas Rolin, Chancellor or the Duchy of Burgundy
249. Graves Region, SW France
250. Lorraine, Eastern France
251. A traditional type of press usually indicates a wine with aspirations to age.
252. Tasmania
253. It appears to increase the amount of Cholesterol ('good cholesterol') in the blood. Other substances in the wine render blood platelets less sticky and therefore less likely to form clots.
254. Troyes, France
255. A water spring used in the making of Glenfiddich Whisky
256. The Duke of Clarence.
257. Madeira
258. The Azores
259. Riesling
260. Pinot Noir
261. South Africa
262. Wallace Beery, James Stewart, Dean Martin, Dudley Moore, Bing Crosby, Ray Milland, Lee Marvin, Jack Lemmon
263. Wilderness, Harvey, Rio Bravo, Arthur, The Country Girl, Lost Weekend, Paint your Wagon, Days of Wine and Roses.
264. Ingrid Bergman, Susan Hayward, Claire Trevor, Joan Fontaine, Claire Bloom, Vivien Leigh, Liz Taylor, Meg Ryan, Judy Garland, Lee Remick
265. Under Capricorn, Smash Up and I'll Cry Tomorrow, Key Largo, Something to Live For, Red Sky at Morning, A Streetcar named Desire, Who's Afraid of Virginia Wolf, When a Man Loves a Woman, Star, Days of Wine and Roses
266. Claret and Whisky
267. Valpolicelli
268. Pas St Martin so named because it is said that St Martin leapt off a rock above the town on to his horse to escape the devil
269. Bellini
270. Brazil. It is made from Cachaca a drink made from raw white spirit similar to Tequila mixed with lemon and sugar
271. Finland
272. Château D'Yquem
273. Their top wines are the Artist Series with labels based on a painting by a different artist each year.
274. Tutankhamen
275. Comes from an early settlement called Christine in honour of Christine Gschwend who was the first white child born in Anderson Valley.
276. Alicante Bouschet because its thick skin withstood transportation.
277. Josephine Tychson at Saint Helena, California in 1886
278. Georgia 5000 to 7000 B.C.
279. Troyes
280. Used by brewers in Stirlingshire to designate the smallest kind of beer in the last century
281. Beer and wine
282. Edradour (120,000 bottles per day approx.)
283. Zurich Switzerland
284. Norwich, England
285. Drambuie
286. Amaretto, the famous Italian liqueur, made from almonds and apricots
287. Birds can't abide the taste of the grape variety Concord which is grown in many vineyards
288. Buckfast Tonic wine made at Buckfast Abbey by the Benedictine monks. It is the favourite drink of dissaffected local

youths in Lanarkshire, Scotland, because it gives them a kick, especially when drunk on top of several cans of strong beer

289. The Moon Under Water
290. Madeira
291. Flanders and Swann
292. Duke Philippe the Bold of Burgundy
293. Adding and mixing a non alcoholic drink to the wine, thereby making a drink of low alcoholic strength.
294. Campaign for Real Ale (set up in 1971)
295. 1919-1933
296. 'Loin de L'Oell' literally meaning far from the eye.
297. Pinotage
298. Tyrconnell. It won the Queen Victoria Plate in 1876 the then Irish Classic
299. Cooley Distillery, Dundalk, Ireland.
300. Beaunois
301. Blauer Zweigelt
302. Henry IV
303. The Armagnac Museum at Condom, SW France
304. Date of distilling and date of bottling
305. Five
306. Turkey
307. From January to March
308 Grenache
309. They are the symbol of romance, health and good fortune
310. Central Victoria, Australia and Napa Valley, California
311. Alexander is a red wine from Coonawarra, Australia
312. Merlot
313. Merlot
314. Gin Gin is a place in the Swan Valley, Australia
315. Yes at Denmark, Frankland River, Australia
316. False
317. Macallan Distillery
318. The Spinning Cone.
319. A code which states that, when a grower dies, the vineyards and estate must be divided equally between his or her children
320. A donkey
321. Glass bottles
322. Armagnac
323. Emu
324. A local supermarket offered it at £1.39 per bottle and were so inundated with demand that that had to ration customers to six bottles each.
325. They were all closed in 1995.
326. Geelong, Victoria, Australia
327. Elizabeth
328. Chardonnay
329. Asbach Brandy
330. Tempranillo
331. Whisky
332. Liebfraumilch.
333. Not exactly but samples from each of 140 Guinness markets worldwide are sent to Ireland to test for quality control
334. An Irish Whiskey
335. Ireland (an Irish Whiskey)
336. Chalon-Sur-Saone, birthplace of Niepce, the celebrated pioneer of photography
337. Trebbiano
338. Jerez, Spain and Champagne, France
339. Kentucky
340. Alsace
341. Juniper Berries
342. Ruby Port, Angostura bitters, grated nutmeg, cloves, oranges.
343. As for 342 but substitute Claret for Ruby Port
344. As for 342 but substitute Champagne for Ruby Port
345. Cork Gin, Angostura bitters and lemon juice
346. Brandy, Madeira, Curacao, Grenadine and the yolk of an egg
347. Bourbon, Gin and Cointreau
348. Whisky Punch is equal quantities of Whisky and water. Hot Toddy is one part Whisky to four parts water although there are variations
349. Beaune
350. Rheims

351. Lily Langtry
352. It's a sweet wine from South Australia.
353. £6,050. A shrapnel patent steel corkscrew sold at Christies
354. A sparkling wine made in Eastern USA made from local grape varieties.
355. Japan
356. Germany (Munich 11th Century)
357. Duchy No. 1 and Duchy No. 3
358. Two Dogs
359. The labels bear a brief resume of people younger than 25 who were seeking their first jobs.
360. Orange, pineapple and cranberry juice.
361. Manzanilla (a dry sherry)
362. Roederer
363. Pomegranate
364. G H Mumm
365. Canary Islands
366. Adult Soft Drinks
367. Banyuls
368. Gigondas
369. Non-alcoholic
370. Literally an enclosure ie. a walled vineyard
371. Lynch-Bages
372. Cattarratto
373. (C) £36,277.
374. The label showed a V for victory.
375. Twenty-four only
376. Tarragona
377. Kenneth McAlpine
378. £2,000,000 (Two million)
379. £46,200
380. £550 approximately per glass.
381. Jersey
382. Rene Firino-Martell
383. Porter originated around 1730 deriving its name from the "Porters" that delivered it
384. A strong ale produced by Shepherd Neame in Kent
385. Orangeboom
386. Labatts Ice Canada
387. SOL the "sun" beer produced in Mexico.
388. The Japanese beer "KIRIN".
389. Cork
390. Pilsen
391. A special weak version of ale known as "small beer".
392. Porter
393. It's an ancient beer first made in 1678, its intense smoky aroma and flavour are the result of malt being cured over smoked beechwood logs
394. Thailand
395. A Chinese grape variety
396. A Turkish red wine
397. A Nemean lion
398. A very particular richness caused by the breakdown of fatty acids in the spirit, after 20 or more years in cask. It is more pronounced in cognac
399. Seyval Blanc.
400. The date of disgorgement
401. Advertising on TV
402. Francis Showering in 1946 at Shepton Mallet, Somerset
403. On the day of birth, a finger dipped in Champagne is rubbed on every newborn baby's lips
404. Stockholm
405. France
406. A measure of Armagnac, local sparkling wine garnished with a slice of orange
407. Corden Park, Cheshire
408. Twenty outlets where alcohol is served
409. Mumm
410. Veuve Clicquot
411. Moet et Chandon
412. Ten
413. Vladivar.
414. Tomato Juice, Horseradish, Celery, Lemon Juice, Lime Juice, Worcestershire Sauce. Tabasco Salt and Pepper, Green Mustard
415. Beef Consomme, spices and flavourings as above (not Tomato Juice or Horseradish)
416. Stands for recently disgorged after the Champagne has spent a long time on its lees
417. Partridge eye - which is pink in colour.
418. Krug

419. False - it is four times more potent.
420. It helps to unmask wines that pretend to be what they are not. It can also detect fraudulent perfumes, coffee, mineral waters, etc.
421. The beer is produced at the first ever Palestinian brewery in a remote Samarian village
422. True
423. Tempranillo
424. Chinon
425. Water (up to 85%).
426. Because its leaves are dusty white underneath
427. Noble Rot (Italian)
428. Coulure
429. Peach juice and iced champagne
430. A rare individually numbered bottle of Macallan Scotch Whisky distilled in 1926 and bottled at 60 years maturity
431. Norway £2.17 (1996)
432. Ugni Blanc
433. Bananas
434. Neumagen-Dhron
435. A cider with the name of Shock
436. He is the Master Distiller for Gordons Gin responsible for its annual production of nearly 50 million litres. His nose determines the quality of the herbs and spices used in its manufacture
437. Twelve people
438. The record is 40 litres made by Dominic Roche in 1996. It took 13 bottles of Irish Whiskey, 6 litres of cream, 1 kg of coffee and 260 spoons of brown sugar to make it
439. Because they were suspicious of wine made by male hands
440. Stromboli
441. 28% proof so as to kill a variety of microbes.
442. To take away the desire for alcohol.
443. Sir Cliff Richard
444. Whiskey/Whisky. The French introduced a weaker (30% alcohol) cheaper imitation
445. Marula, a cream liqueur made from the fruit of the Marula tree (known as elephant tree by the local natives of S. Africa).
446. Chile
447. Green Spot
448. Baron Edmond de Rothschild
449. Murphys Irish Stout
450. Manchester United because a link between hard drink and the players sent completely the wrong message to young supporters
451. Thickhead, a low alcoholic fizzy drink.
452. Château Margaux
453. Champagne manufacturers plan to introduce safety corks which no longer shoot through the air followed by a shower of bubbly.
454. Vodka which will be sold by tax authorities to pay off the tax debt.
455. Veuve Clicquot
456. Bollinger
457. Four. (a) Silver Tequila comes straight from the still. (b) Gold Tequila is silver with flavours primarily caramel. (c) Reposado Tequila has been 'rested' for between two months and a year to mellow it. (d) Anejo Tequila has been aged in Government-sealed oak barrels for at least a year to make it softer and more complex
458. Bollinger 1975 Grand Annee
459. Imran Khan's wedding to Jemima Goldsmith
460. The Gore Brown Trophy
461. 2.5p per bottle
462. £5.77 per bottle
463. Norwich Union
464. Victor Hugo
465. Cutty Sark Whisky offered £1 million to anyone who could capture the Loch Ness Monster.
466. Gamay
467. The strong south easterly wind which blows at the Cape
468. The Douro region of Portugal

469. Gisborne
470. Gisborne
471. The Spanish sombrero and the Porguguese Cape are combined in this elegant figure as homage by Sandeman to the two regions which produce their wines: Jerez and Oporto
472. Gisborne
473. Four years
474. Corn
475. Royal Divorce (Ale)
476. Gaspare Campari an Italian invented the recipe for Campari.
477. 177ft 9ins or (54.18 metres)
478. A dry white wine
479. A medium dry white wine.
480. A white wine
481. Nevers
482. Bubbles in Guinness go down in the glass when every other drink sends its fizz shooting to the surface
483. 1919
484. The return of the Stone of Scone (Dram of Destiny)
485. Chris Patten
486. Cognac
487. The red beer cans which litter the roadsides.
488. Margarita
489. The Rio Casino and Hotel Las Vegas
490. Sheridans Cream Liqueur
491. Château d'Yquem
492. He uses fascist labels on his wine bottles including Adolf Hitler, Mussolini, Lenin, Stalin, etc.
493. (A) Brandy
494. Absinthe
495. The Portman Group
496. A New Zealand white wine made with the grape variety Sauvignon Blanc
497. Mercier
498. Rheims
499. Absinthe
500. Absinthe
501. 80% alcohol
502. Château Lizard is a white wine from Cornwall
503 Jersey, Channel Islands
504. The name derives from the high amount of alcohol consumed with the bottles line up on the table at the end of the meal and the bill calculated by counting from first cork to last
505. He developed a tool which puts an insignia on the bottom of glasses. This activates the gas in the alcohol resulting from a steady stream to the top of the glass without affecting the quality of the drink
506. He broke the French drink driving record when police found him to be seven times over the limit
507. Wine
508. Babycham's bambi-like fawn.
509. Mistletoe
510. Vodka
511. Over 3.6 million pounds
512. Glenfiddich
513. Glenfiddich
514. A Japanese Spirit
515. Glenturret (1775)
516. A 4 year old Whisky (Scottish)
517. Glenfiddich
518. General Marechal Foch
519. The advantages of the health giving properties of red wine appears on the companies bottles.
520. The initiation for all new students at Japanese Universities where they are forced to gulp down pints of alcohol without stopping.
521. Towser was a cat who caught 28,899 mice at a Scottish distillery and is in the Guinness Book of Records.
522. Glenfiddich
523. (C) Amber
524. Lanson
525. Four
526. Kosher wine must be handled by Orthodox, Sabbath-observing Jews from the moment the grapes are crushed to the time it is bottled.
527. Distillery (Dunvills Royal Irish Distillery)

528. An aperitif of sherry, gin and bitters.
529. A device in brewing to prevent spluttering and preventage of waste in barrels.
530. A variety of apple.
531. Toast.
532. (a) The dad is not breaking the law because they will not be drinking in a bar as they are outside (b) The licensee could be committing an offence depending on his knowledge. If he knowingly sells alcohol to someone to deliver it to an under 18 year old he will be breaking the law. But if he didn't know the dad was buying the drink for the boys he wouldn't be committing an offence.
533. Up to now all pints were pumped using the same gas concentration, a 30% Co2 and nitrogen mix. But now, stouts are being pumped with a 25% mix and lagers are bubblier with a 43% gas mix.
534. Up to five extra pints.
535. Hurricane Andrew was to blame for knocking out the cellar's cooling system for five days in 1992. The insurers agreed to an out of court settlement of $2.75 million.
536. The word "punt" which is the hollow at the base of a champagne bottle and the legal currency of Ireland which is also called a punt.
537. Burgundy
538. £8,625.
539. £6,900.
540. Bottles from the Great Nacktarsch, a German vineyard, are labelled with this image.
541. U.S.A.
542. Australia
543. So named because of the view harvesters sometimes enjoyed when looking up the skirts of female colleagues as they bent over to remove bunches of grapes from the vine.
544. Clint Eastwood
545. August 15th 1893
546. Lunch was served inside a 500,000 litre wooden barrel.
547. Highland Park, Orkney Islands.
548. Oban, Talisker, Lagavulin, Dalwhinnie, Craggenmore, Glenkinchie.
549. A QUAICH is a traditional Scottish drinking bowl reserved for tasting the finest single malt whiskies and has been used for centuries.
550. Kinsale the museum is located in Desmond Castle which was formally a customs house.
551. "God Forgive Me"
552. To prevent an Isle of Man company from selling a produce that bears the same name on the label.
553. Queen Anne
554. Brand JINRO DRINK SOJU South Korea
555. Mekhong Thailand
556. Johnny Walker Whisky
557. The date on the bottles labels such as vintage year and the Chateau name.
558. Down and Outs.
559. He was the Worlds oldest student to gain a University Doctorate - his thesis was on the Rhine in Literature.
560. Irish spirit elderflower and sparkling spring water.
561. Glen Kella a re-distilled colourless spirit made on the Isle of Man cannot be called a whisky because it does not comply with the legal definition of the drink.
562. I.G.T. (Indicazione Geografica Tipica)
563. Trevisco Provence North West of Venice.
564. Tia Maria
565. Alice Springs Australia
566. Coonawarra
567. Factors that affect a vine, eg. soil, climate, slope
568. Northern
569. George Best
570. The World's first Black Whisky called "Loch Dhu"
571. (C) Celtic Crossing

572. This is the name given to the product of the first distillation in the pot still process of whiskey manufacture
573 Gloria
574 Poison foot after several toe amputations
575 Yeast
576 Fats Waller
577 Hops used in Beer
578 Cocktails
579 Scottish
580 George Washington
581 Tolly Cobbold, Ipswich
582 One "The Tottenham" built 1892 and is a listed building
583 Cava
584 India
585 Intelligent
586 The drunkometer was introduced in 1938 in Indianapolis
587 Thailand
588 He set a new drink driving record after being convicted for being over the limit for the eighth time in three years
589 Napoleon Brandy
590 Chasselas
591 She emptied a bath full of Mumm champagne in their hotel suite in error.
592 Ferintosh
593 Can be used to remove sediment in champagne
594 Illinois USA
595 Used to treat heavy drinkers who are alcohol dependent, it acts directly to limit craving
596 St Émilion (A subterranean church built under the town square)
597 Ireland (12.8%)
598 The harvest time - can also mean the year in which a wine is made
599 The blending of wine of the same origin to create a cuvée or blend
600 Drunkenness

FRANCE

1. Appellation d'Origine Controlee means controlled place name and a guide to the origin and authenticity of any wine whose label bears these letters
2. Vins Delimites de Qualite Superieure - Second from top category of French wines which are strictly regulated
3. Local or country wine which offer individuality of style and are subject to strict controls - these wines are third in classification of French wines
4. Vin de table is the lowest category of French wines
5. Nouveau
6. Bottled
7. A wine shipper-merchant who buys wine after it is made, matures it in his cellars, bottles it when it is ready and then ships it abroad.
8. The wines are matured on their lees ie. the residue or deposit left in the cask and placed into bottles without first racking
9. A white wine made from black grapes.
10. A large barrel/cask
11. The empty space above the liquid in either a cask or a bottle between the wine and the closure of the container
12. Eugene Charmot developed a technique at the beginning of the 20th century whereby a quality sparkling wine may be made in large sealed tanks rather than in bottles thereby reducing the production costs by saving time, money and labour
13. A yellow wine from the Jura district of France made from Sauvignon grape. The yellow colour is obtained from a flor which settles on the wine which is matured for a period of six years
14. Built as a charitable hospital for the poor in the fifteenth century. Owns many fine vineyards. Its wines are auctioned in November in Beaune and the proceeds are used for the upkeep of the hospital

15. The widow of a French wine producer called Ponsardin and is credited with inventing remuage and degorgement of champagne
16. Alsace
17. French Queen. Married Henry II of England in 1152 AD and for 300 years the vineyards of Bordeaux and surrounding areas were under English control
18. Hermitage
19. Midi
20. Region in the Rhône area of France
21. Third (1937)
22. Six. Gard, Ardeche, Drome, Loire, Rhône and Vaucluse
23. Tavel Rosé
24. Rhône
25. Beaujolais
26. True
27. It is released for sale on the third Thursday of November
28. 1973
29. A district in the Lot-et-Garonne department of SW France
30. Chinon and Bourgeuil
31. Loire
32. Avignon
33. Pope Clement V
34. Northern Rhône
35. St. Vincent
36. The shaking and turning of each bottle of champagne during its secondary fermentation in a special rack known as a pupitre over a period of several weeks. This allows the sediment to settle against the cork when the bottles are upside down and ready for degorgement.
37. Claret
38. A dry white wine from the central vineyard of the Loire
39. A dry white wine from the Maconnaise in Southern Burgundy
40. A white grape variety also known as the Chenin Blanc
41. Côtes d'Or, a top wine area of Burgundy
42. Medoc. The top district of Bordeaux on the west bank of the river Gironde
43. Côtes Blonde and Côte Brune. The legend supposedly stems from a medieval lord who in his will divided his vineyards between his two daughters, one blonde and the other brunette
44. A very strong cold wind that blows down the Rhône Valley
45. An area of the Cognac region strictly controlled by law
46. Cognac Region
47. Very Superior Old Pale used on labels of some bottles of Cognac
48. Made in the Gers department of SW France.
49. Name given to the evaporation of a spirit which takes place whilst it is maturing in cask.
50. Evaporation of Cognac through porous wood barrels into the atmosphere during maturing
51. A bottle of 3 star brandy must be aged for at least two years
52. 4 years
53. 6 years
54. Cognac is aged in barrels made from oak trees grown in Limousin
55. Superior
56. Gewürztraminer
57. Spicey
58. Armagnac Brandy Region
59. Red Burgundy
60. Narbonne to the Spanish border (Corbieres, Fitou, Minervois, Roussillon)
61. Sung by Maurice Chevalier in the film "Gigi"
62. Julienas in the Beaujolais Region.
63. Baron Philippe de Rothschild commissions an artist for Château Mouton-Rothschild
64. Pablo Picasso, John Huston, Cesar, Bona, Joan Miro, Andy Warhol, Arman, Hans Hartung, Salvador Dali, Hisao Domoto, Pierre Soulages, etc.
65. Jura
66. The Mercier champagne cellars which extend underground for over 11 miles.

67. One of the largest barrels in the world with a capacity of 200,000 bottles
68. The Popes mitre above the crossed keys of the Kingdom of Heaven

ITALY

1. A mild sweet wine
2. Very sweet
3. A medium sweet wine
4. Asti is a town in the Piedmont region
5. Centre of vermouth production in Italy.
6. Asti Spumante, Barolo, Barbaresco, Barbera, Spanna, Carema, Grignolino, Gavi etc.
7. Soave, Barolino, Piave, Valpolicella, etc.
8. Emilia-Romagna
9. A red wine produced in the Valtellina
10. Dry
11. Yes
12. Red wine
13. A harsh brandy produced from the residue after the grape juice has been removed
14. None, they all produce wine
15. To sparkle or to foam
16. The term defines the wine as coming from the very heart of the area of production
17. Wines for which the storage period has been officially laid down and which therefore cannot be sold before expiry of this period
18. Slightly sparkling
19. The grape is named after a river
20. UK
21. Veneto Region
22. Calabria in Southern Italy
23. Chianti Classico (Central region only)
24. Chianti Putto (a consortium of six outer regions)
25. Sardinia
26. Sicily
27. A colourless liqueur made from aniseed and made in Italy
28. Emilia-Romagna
29. Emilia-Romagna
30. Cinqueterre wine
31. Muscat grape variety
32. Taurasi
33. Sangiovese, Trebbiano, Canaiolo Nero and Malvasia del Chianti
34. Made from the grape of the same name in Tuscany
35. Turin
36. DOCG
37. Lachryma Christi del Vesuvio
38. 1963
39. Asti Spumante
40. Sicily
41. Mosto Cotto is a reduced wine by slow cooking to approximately half of its original amount and is used to give colour and flavour to Marsala wine
42. Liguria
43. Emilia-Romagna
44. Torgiano
45. Nebbiolo
46. Romulus and Remus with the she wolf on its neck label.
47. Piedmont
48. Latium
49. Umbria
50. Lombardy

GERMANY

1. Rhine and Rhône
2. Noble rot - a fungus which attacks grapes in mild and moist conditions.
3. Yes, but only account for about 10% to 15% of the total
4. Saar, Mosel, Neckar, Main, Ruwer.
5. Tafelwein
6. Qualitatswein mit Pradikat
7. 1879
8. Green
9. Brown
10. Most come from the Rheinhesse. German wine law simply says it must be a good quality Rheinish wine
11. Hock named after the Rhine wine Hochheimer
12. Trier
13. Red wines
14. Mosel

15. Rudesheim
16. Asbach brandy
17. Red wine
18. Top selling Liebfraumilch wine.
19. Lorelei
20. Dry wine
21. An area or region specifically defined by German wine laws
22. Literally ice wine picked while water content of ripened grapes are frozen
23. German system for measuring the amount of sugar in a must.
24. Yes
25. Germany is the most northerly of the main wine producing countries of Europe
26. It is the name given to a single vineyard as defined by the German wine laws of 1971
27. Grosslage is the German for large vineyard which according to the 1971 wine laws must include a number of individual vineyards and whose character must produce wines of a similar quality
28. QMP quality wine which has no sugar added to the must and is estate bottled.
29. QMP wine grapes gathered after the official harvest date have a higher sugar content
30. QMP sweet wine, a noble growth - grapes are selected and separated from any imperfect or unripe grapes
31. QMP sweet wine made from over ripe grapes which have been affected by noble rot
32. QMP rich sweet wine made from selected shrivelled grapes which have been attacked by noble rot
33. Rheinpfalz, also known as the Palatinate.
34. Hessische Bergstrasse (the wines are not exported)
35. The quality control number. Every QMP and QBA wine is allocated a number which indicates where the wine was tested, bottled by whom and when
36. St. Urban
37. Sparkling
38. An estate
39. There are eleven designated regions for Germany's quality wines
40. Baden, Franken, Hessische, Bergstrasse, Mitterlhein, Mosel-Saar-Ruwer, Nahe, Rheingau, Rheinpfalz, Wurttemberg, Ahr
41. Between 10-15%
42. Minimum of 85%
43. Rheingau
44. Moselle

SPAIN AND PORTUGAL

1. A refreshing drink made from wine (usually red), slices of lemon and orange, sugar and aerated water
2. Red
3. Top level quality of red wines which must have been allowed to age in casks for two years followed by three more years in the bottle
4. A veil of wine yeast peculiar to sherry. The veil protects the sherry from the harmful effects of the air
5. Aged wines which cannot be sold until they have spent at least twelve months ageing in casks
6. A cellar or wine shop
7. A vine
8. System of producing sherry. Butts of older wine are systematically topped up with younger wine of similar style which in turn are refreshed from even younger casks and so on. The number of scales vary but rarely less than five or six
9. Manzanilla, Lightest and palest, very dry. Fino, Straw colour, slightly less dry than Manzanilla. Amontillado, Dry wine but older. Oloroso, Medium dry
10. Ebro
11. Andalucia, Aragon, Castilla-Leon, Castilla-la-Mancha, Cataluna, Galicia, Levante, Navarra, Rioja
12. No. (Palomino IS)

13. A system of classification for types of sherry
14. Bodega
15. The nursery where the younger sherries are kept waiting to enter the solera system
16. Dry, Medium, Sweet
17. Red - Rioja Navarra etc.
    White - Navarra, Rioja, etc.
    Sparkling - Cava, Penedes
18. Majorca
19. Jerez de la Frontera
20. Palomino
21. Sercial, Verdelho, Bual, Malmsey
22. Best known are Malvasia, Mourisco, Tinta Roriz, Tinta Francesca, Tinta Cao, Touriga
23. Portuguese word for "hot house" where Madeira wine is held to give it the special cooked flavour
24. A vineyard estate
25. Wooden troughs where grapes are pressed
26. Ruby, Tawny, White, Vintage, Late Bottled Vintage, Off Vintage, Vintage Character
27. Red wines can only be called reserva when they have undergone a period of one year's ageing in oak cask followed by two years in bottle
28. The wine is made with at least 85% of grapes picked in the year quoted on the label
29. Agramont, Camponuevo, Navarra white and red wine
30. Montilla
31. Sercial, a pale dry white wine
32. Verdelho, a darker medium dry wine.
33. Bual, slightly darker in colour but sweeter than Verdelho
34. Malmsey, a sweet wine
35. Colares
36. Tarragona
37. Duke of Clarence
38. NW Portugal between Douro and Minho
39. DAO
40. Named after the local clay soil barro.
41. A treaty signed in 1703 giving the wines of Portugal preferential taxation over that for French wines
42. Spain and Portugal

SPARKLING WINE

1. Champagne
2. Four bottles
3. Magnum
4. 75% approximately
5. Pinot Noir, Pinot Meunier, Chardonnay
6. 7-9 degrees C. Below it loses its fragrance, warmer it becomes heavy and loses its sparkle
7. Blanc de Blanc
8. Of one exclusive year
9. Blended from the wines of several years
10. Two
11. Rheims, Ay, Epernay, Bouzy, Hautvillers, etc.
12. Secondary fermentation in the bottle, the carbonnic acid gas produced by this fermentation is absorbed by the liquid under pressure and when the cork is drawn, will cause the wine to sparkle
13. The sediment is removed by a technique called degorging. The bottles are very lightly shaken and twisted to bring them to an almost inverted position which allows the sediment to settle in the neck of the bottle. The bottles are then placed into a freezing mixture which will freeze it. The top is removed allowing the gas to force the sediment out
14. The amount of wine lost in degorging is replaced by a measured amount of sweetened wine (dosage)
15. In champagne area it means that less yeast and sugar were added to the wine to produce champagne which means that there is only approximately half the normal gas pressure
16. Moet et Chandon, Mumms, Krug Bollinger, Pol Roger, Lanson, Charles Heidsieck Tattinger, Veuve Clicquot-Ponsardin, Laurent Perrier, etc.
17. Non vintage

18. Pol Roger
19. Semi sparkling wine
20. Germany
21. Asti Spumante, Moscato d'Asti
22. Cava, Penedes
23. Blanquette de Limoux, Saumur, Touraine, etc.
24. A flute
25. Noel Coward
26. 6.34kg/cm2 approximately
27. Marne, Vesle, Aube, Aisne
28. Brut
29. Doux or Demi-sec
30. Semi sparkling wine
31. Chalk and rock
32. Yes. Bouzy
33. Benedictine
34. Nicole-Clicquot-Ponsardin
35. Moet et Chandon
36. Winston Churchill
37. Most will benefit from up to 3 years before drinking
38. (A) Cooled slowly by placing the bottle in a mixture of ice and water for 30 minutes
    (B) 1-2 hours in a refrigerator
    (C) Rapid ice vacuvin coolers for 5 minutes
39. Methode Champenoise, Charmat or Tank method, Transfer method and Carbonation
40 Yes, Coteaux Champenois
41. Vintage, Shipper, Champagne
42. Rosé made by blending white and red wines
43. Six bottles
44. Sixteen bottles
45. Twelve bottles
46. Eight bottles
47. A firm's finest wine
48. The name given to sparkling cider.
49. 50% Champagne and 50% Guinness served chilled in a pint or half pint tankard
50. A song sung in Victorian times.
51. Loire
52. Twenty bottles
53. Tank or Charmat method
54. Agrafe
55. A Cellarman
56. There would be too much sugar and colour in the grape
57. Beau Brummell
58. The journalist Jeffrey Bernard who judges champagne
59. That the name on the label is not the producer's, but a name chosen by the seller of the wine
60. The champagne is made by the grower and is not from a champagne house.
61. Produced by the champagne house indicated on the label
62. Ayala (1963)

TRUE OR FALSE

1. FALSE
2. TRUE
3. TRUE
4. TRUE
5. TRUE
6. FALSE
7. FALSE
8. TRUE
9. TRUE
10. TRUE
11. FALSE
12. TRUE
13. FALSE
14. FALSE
15. FALSE
16. TRUE
17. TRUE
18. TRUE
19. FALSE
20. FALSE
21. TRUE
22. FALSE
23. TRUE
24. FALSE
25. TRUE
26. TRUE
27. TRUE
28. FALSE
29. FALSE
30. TRUE
31. FALSE
32. TRUE
33. FALSE
34. FALSE
35. FALSE
36. TRUE
37. FALSE
38. FALSE
39. TRUE
40. FALSE
41. TRUE
42. FALSE
43. FALSE
44. TRUE
45. TRUE
46. TRUE
47. FALSE
48. TRUE
49. TRUE
50 TRUE
51. TRUE
52. FALSE
53. TRUE
54. TRUE
55. FALSE
56. FALSE
57. FALSE
58. FALSE
59. FALSE
60. FALSE
61. TRUE
62. FALSE
63. TRUE
64. TRUE
65. TRUE
66. FALSE
67. FALSE
68. TRUE
69. FALSE
70 TRUE
71. TRUE
72. FALSE
73. TRUE
74. TRUE
75. TRUE
76. FALSE
77. TRUE
78. FALSE
79. FALSE
80. FALSE
81. TRUE
82. TRUE
83. TRUE
84. FALSE
85. FALSE
86. FALSE
87. TRUE
88. TRUE
89. FALSE
90. FALSE
91. TRUE
92. TRUE
93. TRUE
94. FALSE
95. FALSE
96. TRUE
97. TRUE
98. TRUE
99. FALSE
100. FALSE
101. FALSE
102. FALSE
103. TRUE
104. TRUE
105. FALSE
106. FALSE
107. TRUE
108. TRUE
109. TRUE
110. TRUE
111. FALSE
112. TRUE
113. TRUE
114. TRUE
115. FALSE
116. FALSE
117. TRUE
118. TRUE
119. TRUE
120. TRUE
121 TRUE

DRINK - HEALTH AND LEGAL

1. 90 litres of still wine or 60 litres of sparkling wine. In addition we can also import 20 litres of fortified wine, 10 litres of spirits and 110 litres of beer.
2. 35 microgrammes of alcohol.
3. 107 milligrammes of alcohol.
4. Yes, they are obliged to serve tap water if not they could be refused a liquor licence.
5. 8
6. One hour
7. 100 calories approximately.
8. True
9. (a) How much you drink
   (b) Whether you have eaten recently
   (c) Your size
   (d) Your age
   (e) Male or female
10. 4 hour approximately
11. False. The body actually loses heat.
12. (a) Imprisonment or heavy fine (or both if you cause death by careless driving while under the influence of drink or drugs).
    (b) Disqualification from driving for a period
13. 5 years
14. (a) criminal record
    (b) loss of driving licence
    (c) reputation suffers
    (d) family life affected
    (e) loss of personal transport
15. (a) possible job loss
    (b) increase in travelling expenses
    (c) inconvenience
    (d) court fine
    (e) legal expenses
    (f) increased insurance premiums
16. Serving a quantity of drink over the permitted level.
17. One litre of alcoholic drink exceeding 22% vol. plus two litres of still wine, or Two litres of alcoholic drink (other than still wine) and not exceeding 22% vol. plus two litres of still wine.
18. When travelling between EC countries you are entitled to your full duty free allowance on each and every journey on your way out and on your way back. Passengers can now take home double the previous limits.
19. No
20. Sweden
21. Portugal
22. It allows children under 14 years and accompanied by an adult into a pub.
23. (a) that the bar area is suitable for children and has a family atmosphere.
    (b) meals and soft drinks must be available during the period set aside in the children's area.
    (c) The certificate should operate between ll am and 9 pm.
24. 3 x 330ml cans of beer or 3 x 20cl wine.
25. 1970
26. 45 litres still wine of which only
    30 litres can be sparkling wine
    20 litres fortified wine
    55 litres beer
    10 litres spirits.

Part 2

Drinks Teasers

GRAPE VARIETIES

1. PINOT NOIR
2. GAMAY
3. CHARDONNAY
4. NEBBIOLO
5. PALOMINO
6. SHIRAZ
7. PINOT MEUNIER
8. ZINFANDEL
9. RIESLING
10. MERLOT
11. CABERNET FRANC
12. TREBBIANO
13. TEMPRANILLO
14. BARBERA
15. CABERNET SAUVIGNON
16. SEMILLON
17. SAUVIGNON BLANC
18. CHENIN BLANC
19. GRENACHE
20. CINSAULT
21. SILVANER
22. MULLER-THURGAU
23. ALIGOTE
24. VIOGNIER
25. MALVASIA

Jumbled Drinks

1. MEURSAULT
2. GLENLIVET
3. LAMBRUSCO
4. HAUT BRION
5. ALTO ADIGE
6. HAWKES BAY
7. FRANCONIA
8. INGLENOOK
9. BUSHMILLS
10. MOONSHINE
22. BARDOLINO
12. NEGOTIANT
13. ST ÉMILION
14. RUDESHEIM
15. TARTRATES
16. ST RAPHAEL
17. CÔTE BRUNE
18. COINTREAU
19. LANGUEDOC
20. CORKSCREW
21. CLOS DU ROI
22. HERMITAGE
23. SAUTERNES
24. CHAMPAGNE
25. CUVE CLOSE
26. CÔTE RÔTIE
27. BOURGEUIL
28. FORTIFIED
29. AUSTRALIA
30. SAUVIGNON
31. SENANCOLE
32. SLIVOVITZ

RE-ARRANGE THE FOLLOWING GROUPS TO FORM WINES

	JUMBLED	CORRECT WORD	EXTRA LETTER	NEW WORD
1	CARNOGC	COGNAC	R	
	AOVSES	SOAVE	S	
	ALGAMEA	MALAGA	E	
	CAMOUN	MACON	U	
	TARETCIL	CLAIRET	T	
	PITHANCI	CHIANTI	P	PETRUS
2	MALACNIPO	PALOMINO	C	
	LOCNAM	MACON	L	
	WAEINESE	EISWEIN	A	
	EOAD	DAO	E	
	BIHLTSAC	CHABLIS	T	
	SADNOGIGR	GIGONDAS	R	CLARET
3	AHEVLT	TAVEL	H	
	MURSYAU	SAUMUR	Y	
	ARAMSRAL	MARSALA	R	
	NIXIFA	FIXEN	A	
	CADMUSSTE	MUSCADET	S	SYRAH
4	RLOMEPRO	POMEROL	R	
	LOYYANV	VOLNAY	Y	
	AAGSALM	MALAGA	S	
	RAHMDEEIA	MADEIRA	H	
	SAFERAMA	MARSALA	E	
	ARAGROTRAN	TARRAGONA	R	SHERRY
5	RSEBMUAUTL	MERSAULT	B	
	RUARENSNEC	SANCERRE	U	
	ORNNHIC	CHINON	R	
	LOGBNDA	BANDOL	G	
	NYUSTEANA	SANTENAY	U	
	LYNABE	BLAYE	N	
	DLERULYI	REULLY	D	
	YLMOES	MOSEL	Y	BURGUNDY
6	RSABREBA	BARBERA	S	
	VRYOAUVI	VOUVRAY	I	
	NIENCRDOU	CONDRIEU	N	
	VESAOV	SOAVE	V	
	TUAFOI	FITOU	A	VISAN

Wine Words

Can you fill in the missing spaces?

STYLE	**France**	**Italy**	**Spain**	**Germany**	**Portugal**	**Yugoslavia**	**Hungary**
White	Blanc	Bianco	Blanco	Weiss	Branco	Bijelo	Feher
Red	Rouge	Rosso	Tinto	Rotwein	Tinto	Crno	Voros
Sparkling	Mousseux	Spumante	Espumoso	Sekt	Espumante	Biser	Habzo
Dry	Sec/Brut	Secco	Seco	Trocen	Seco	Suho	Szaraz
Sweet	Doux	Dolce	Dulce	Suss	Adamado/Doce	Slatko	Edes
Rosé	Rosé	Rosato	Rosado	Rotling	Rosado	Ruzica	Roze

Odd One Out

Each group of words has one word out of place, which one does not belong and why?

St Émilion	St Estèphe	St Julien	**St Péray**
Anjou	Tavel	**Mateus**	Touraine
Grappa	**Cognac**	Marc	Aguardiente
Curacao	**Calvados**	Grand Marnier	Cointreau
Pomerol	Fronsac	St Émilion	**Morgon**
Bougeuil	Cornas	Hermitage	Gigondas
Bahai	Kahlua	Tia Maria	**Sambuca**
Malmsey	Bual	Sercial	**Marsala**
Fino	**Tawny**	Amontillado	Manzanilla
Pinot Noir	**Chardonnay**	Shiraz	Gamay
Minervois	**Malmsey**	Macon	Montrachet
Pernod	**Ouzo**	Pastis	Ricard
Evian	Vittel	**Perrier**	Contrexeville
Fraise	Framboise	Grenadine	**Gomme**
Fleurie	Brouilly	Chenas	**Barsac**
Gironde	Garonne	**Saone**	Dordogne
Bardolino	Soave	Valpolicella	**Orvieto**
Penedes	Valdepenas	Montilla	**Bairrada**
Asti Spumante	Bardolino	Chianti	Orvieto

Miscellaneous

RIVER	REGION
MURRAY	SOUTH AUSTRALIA
DARLING	BRISBANE
HUDSON	NEW YORK
COLUMBIA	WASHINGTON, USA
SANTA MARGARITA	SOUTHERN CALIFORNIA
ESTRELLA	MONTEREY, USA
SALINAS	MONTEREY, USA
RUSSIAN	SONOMA COUNTY, USA
MOULOUYA	MOROCCO
OSAM	BULGARIA
MURA	YUGOSLAVIA
OHRE	CZECHOSLOVAKIA
DOURO	PORTUGAL
RIO LIMA	PORTUGAL
FRANCOLI	CATALONIA, SPAIN
EBRO	SPAIN
SACCO	SOUTHERN ITALY
TEVERE	ITALY
LIESER	MOSEL, GERMANY
GOLO	CORSICA
ISERE	RHÔNE, FRANCE
DOUBS	JURA, FRANCE
TET	ROUSSILLION, FRANCE
WEISS	ALSACE
GOULBURN	VICTORIA, AUSTRALIA
LAHN	KOBLENZ, GERMANY
BODROG	HUNGARY
MARCIA	BULGARIA
DROPT	CÔTE DE DURAS
PO	ITALY
TARA	YUGOSLAVIA
BAISE	FRANCE
OJA	SPAIN

Odd One Out

St. Péray is a Rhône wine,
the others are Bordeaux wines.

Mateus is a Portuguese wine,
the others are French wines.

Cognac is a top quality brandy,
the others are not.

Calvados is an apple brandy,
the others are orange flavoured.

Morgon is a wine from Burgundy,
the others are from Bordeaux.

Bourgueil is a wine from the Loire,
the others are from the Rhône.

Sambuca is aniseed flavour,
the others are coffee flavoured.

Marsala is an Italian wine,
the others are types of Madeira.

Tawny is a port wine,
the others are types of sherry.

Chardonnay is a white grape,
the others are red.

Malmsey is a Maderia wine,
the others are white wines.

Ouzo is colourless,
the others are yellow in colour.

Perrier is a sparkling water,
the others are still.

Gomme is a clear syrup,
the others are red.

Barsac is a Bordeaux wine,
the others are from Burgundy.

Saone is a river in Burgundy,
the others are in Bordeaux.

Orvieto is a wine from Umbria,
the others are from Veneto.

Bairrada is a wine from Portugal,
the others come from Spain.

Asti-Spumante is a sparkling wine,
the others are still wines.

Jumbled Triangles

	WINE	EXTRA LETTER		WINE	EXTRA LETTER
1	Champagne	R	19	Côte Brune	N
2	Zinfandel	A	20	Bardonino	O
3	Edelfaule	L	21	Hautbrion	R
4	Tramminer	O	22	Bourgueil	O
5	Pinot Noir	R	23	Champagne	M
6	St Emilion	O	24	Hermitage	G
		BAROLO			MORGON
7	Haut Brion	M	25	Chautagny	R
8	Meursault	A	26	Montlouis	A
9	Bourgogne	L	27	Corbieres	B
10	Macon Rosé	A	28	Costieres	C
11	Knipperle	G	29	Languedoc	A
12	Quintigny	A	30	Steinberg	S
		MALAGA			BARSAC
13	Lambrusco	C	31	Montravel	L
14	St. Estèphe	N	32	Bourgeois	O
15	Chasselas	N	33	Chatillon	N
16	Minervois	H	34	Monthelie	D
17	Bardolino	O	35	Irouleguy	B
18	Tarragona	I	36	Vincelles	A
		CHINON			BANDOL

HOW MANY SONGS/MUSIC CAN YOU NAME WITH DRINK IN ITS TITLE?

Days of Wine and Roses
Little Old Wine Drinker Me
The Night they Invented Champagne
Seven Drunken Nights
Drink to me Only
Mistletoe and Wine
Red Red Wine
Applejack
On my Lips every Kiss is like Wine
Come and have a drink
What shall we do with the drunken sailor
Wine Women and Song
A glass of champagne
Whiskey in the Jar
Champagne Galop
Rum and Coca Cola
Drink Drink
Champagne Polka
Madeira
Summer Wine

Answers

The Lady Drinks Champagne
Whisky River
Cigarettes and Alcohol
Whiskey on a Sunday
Pub with no Beer
Juice of the Barley
The Moonshiner
Kisses Sweeter than Wine
Lilac Wine

Cocktails

NAME THE INGREDIENTS IN THE COCKTAILS LISTED:

Between the Sheets - Brandy, White Rum, Cointreau, Lemon Juice

Bucks Fizz - Champagne, Fresh Orange Juice

Blue Lady - Blue Curacao, Gin, Lemon Juice, Egg White

Bronx - Gin, Vermouth, Orange Juice

Brooklyn - Rye Whiskey, Sweet Vermouth, Maraschino, Amer Picon

Chocolate Soldier - Brandy, Dry Vermouth, Creme de Cacao, Orange, Bitters.

Daiquiri - White Rum, Fresh Lime Juice, Gomme Syrup

First Night - Brandy, Van der Hum, Tia Maria, Fresh Cream

Gin and It - Gin, Sweet Vermouth

Grand Slam - Dry Vermouth, Sweet Vermouth, Swedish Punch

Harvey Wallbanger - Vodka, Orange Juice, Galliano

Honeymoon - Benedictine, Applejack Brandy, Lemon Juice, Orange Curacao

London Fog - White Creme de Menthe, Anisette, Angostura Bitters

Maidens Prayer - Gin, Cointreau, Orange Juice, Lemon Juice

Manhatten - Rye Whiskey, Vermouth, Angostura Bitters

Maple Leaf - Bourbon Whiskey, Fresh Lemon Juice, Maple Syrup

Paradise - Gin, Apricot Brandy, Orange Juice

Pink Lady - Gin, Grenadine, Egg White

Rusty Nail - Scotch Whisky, Drambuie

San Francisco - Sloe Gin, Italian Vermouth, French Vermouth, Angostura Orange Bitters

White Lady - Gin, Cointreau, Lemon Juice

Shirley Temple/Roy Rogers - Ginger Ale, Dash of Grenadine

Jump up and Kiss me - White Rum, Apricot Brandy, Galliano, Lemon Juice, Pineapple Juice, Egg White

Speciality Coffees

NAME THE SPIRIT IN THE COFFEES LISTED:

Monks - Benedictine
Gaelic - Irish Whiskey
Seville - Orange Liqueur
Russian - Vodka
Mexican - Tequilla
French - Brandy
Jamaican - Rum
Calypso - Tia Maria
Witches - Strega
Kentucky/Mississippi - Southern Comfort
Flamenco - Orange Curacao
Bonnie Prince Charlie - Drambuie
Scotch Mist - Glayva
Highlander - Taleskar Malt Whisky

French Regions

CÔTES DU RHÔNE	1
PROVENCE	2
CHAMPAGNE	3
LOIRE	4
LOIRE	5
CÔTES DE NUITS BURGUNDY	6
CÔTES DE NUITS BURGUNDY	7
ALSACE	8
BORDEAUX	9
BORDEAUX	10
PROVENCE	11
LANGUEDOC MIDI	12
BEAUJOLAIS BURGUNDY	13
CÔTES DE BEAUNE BURGUNDY	14
LOIRE	15
CÔTES DU RHÔNE	16
CÔTES DU RHÔNE	17
BERGERAC DORDOGNE	18
BORDEAUX	19
BORDEAUX	20
LANGUEDOC MIDI	21
LOIRE	22
PROVENCE	23
JURA	24
CÔTES DU RHÔNE	25

Liqueurs

HOW MUCH DO YOU REALLY KNOW ABOUT LIQUEURS/

1 Ouzo, Aniseed/herbs, Greece
2 Sabra, Orange Chocolate, Israel
3 Tia Maria, Coffee, Jamaica
4 Baileys Irish Cream , Cream/Chocolate, Ireland
5 Crême de Kirsch, Cherries, Italy/ Yugoslavia/Switzerland
6 Chartreuse, Herbs/Bark, France
7 Advocaat, Egg Yolks, Holland
8 Amaretto, Almond/Apricot Kernals, Italy
9 Southern Comfort, Peach/Citrus Fruit, USA
10 Galliano, Herbs/Flowers/Roots, Italy
11 Curacao, Bitter Orange Peel, France/ Holland
12 Irish Mist, Herbs/Honey, Ireland
13Drambuie, Herbs/Honey, Scotland
14 Benedictine D.O.M, Herbs/Bark, France
15 Sambuca, Elderberries/Liquorice, Italy
16 Izzara, Elderberries/Herbs, Spain
17 Bronte, Honey/Herbs, England
18 Cassis, Blackcurrants, France
19 Parfait Amour, Citrus/Violets/Vanilla Rosewater France/Holland
20 Kummel, Aniseed/Cumin/Carraway, Germany/Holland
21 Cointreau, Oranges, France
22 Midori, Melon, Japan
23 Bahia, Coffee, Brazil
24 Edelweiss, Herbs/Twigs, Italy
25 Glayva, Herbs/Spices, Scotland
26 Mirabelle, Plums, France
27 Aurum, Citrus/Spices/Herbs, Italy/France
28 Grand Marnier, Oranges, France
29 Maraschino, Cherries, Italy/Yugoslavia
30 Van der Hum, Bark/Tangerines, South Africa

Italian Regions

LATIUM	1
TUSCANY	2
PIEDMONT	3
SICILY	4
MARCHES	5
VENETO	6
VENETO	7
LATIUM	8
SICILY	9
UMBRIA	10
VENETO	11
CAMPANIA	12
LOMBARDY	13
EMILIA-ROMAGNA	14
PIEDMONT	15
PIEDMONT	16
VENETO	17
PIEDMONT	18
CAMPANIA	19
CAMPANIA	20
CALABRIA	21
SICILY	22

PIEDMONT	23
LIGURIA	24
APULIA	25

Quotations

1 G B Shaw
2 Napoleon
3 Pasteur
4 Oscar Wilde
5 Rudyard Kipling
6 James Stewart in the film "The Philadelphia Story"
7 Peter Langan
8 Dr Samuel Johnson 1780
9 Martin Luther
10 Lord Byron
11 Robert Louis Stevenson
12 K Livingstone 1945
13 Anthony Powell 1905
14 Logan Peasall Smith 1865-1946
15 Isak Dinesen (Karen Blixen) 1885-1962
16 Clarke 1639
17 Robert Burton 1577-1640
18 Voltaire
19 St Jerome
20 Mark Twain
21 Robert Louis Stevenson
22 Robert Louis Stevenson
23 Robert Burns
24 Rousseau
25 Confucius
26 Poupon
27 Euripide
28 V Hugo
29 Lilly Bollinger
30, 31, 32, 33 Confucius
34 Ulster MP Rev. Ian Paisley (Discussing Draught Guinness)
35 Robert Burns

Drinks used in dishes

1 Trifle Aux Xeres, Sherry
2 Zabaglione, Marsala
3 Crepe Suzette, Brandy and Curacao
4 Coupe Jamaique, Rum
5 Bombe Aida, Kirsch
6 Coupe Andalouse, Maraschino or Curacao
7 Bombe Clicquot, Champagne
8 Coupe Elizabeth, Cherry Brandy
9 Coupe Eugene, Maraschino
10 Zuccotto, Brandy and Maraschino
11 Tiramisu, Tia Maria
12 Souffle Grand Marnier, Grand Marnier
13 Baked Alaska, Kirsch
14 Flummery, White Wine - Sherry .
15 Tripe a la Caen, Champagne
16 Tournedo Rossini, Madeira
17 Chicken Chasseur, Dry White Wine
18 Entrecote Marchand de Vin, Red Wine
19 Welsh Rarebit, Beer
20 Carbonnade of Beef, Beer
21 Lobster Bisque, Brandy
22 Fondue, White Wine
23 Lemon Posset, Dry White Wine
24 Banana Flambe, Rum or Brandy
25 Steak Diane, Brandy
26 Turtle Soup, Dry Sherry
27 Strawberries Romanoff, Curacao - Grand Marnier
28 Scampi Provencale, Dry White Wine
29 Lobster Thermidor, Dry White Wine
30 Beef Bourguignonne, Burgundy Wine
31 Athol Brose, Whisky

Proverbs and Toasts

To break the code substitute the following letters

B C D E F G H I J K L M N O P Q R S T U V W X Y Z A with

A B C D E F G H I J K L M N O P Q R S T U V W X Y Z

Therefore the answer to Question number 1 is

PORT IS THE CURE FOR ALL ILLS EXCEPT DEATH

Now you complete the remainder.

Polybius Squares

1 CHINON
FRASCATI
CHIANTI
BAROLO
RIESLING
MORGON
FIXIN
GAMAY
EST EST EST
CHAMPAGNE

2 GRAND MARNIER
IRISH MIST
CURACAO
KAHLUA
KUMMEL
STREGA
TIA MARIA
MARASCHINO
DRAMBUIE
CRÊME DE MENTHE

Key Number Ciphers

A

2	4	5	1	3
S	**E**	**R**	**V**	**E**
R	**E**	**D**	**W**	**I**
N	**E**	**W**	**I**	**T**
H	**G**	**A**	**M**	**E**

B

2	4	5	1	3
F	**I**	**N**	**O**	**I**
S	**A**	**V**	**E**	**R**
Y	**D**	**R**	**Y**	**S**
H	**E**	**R**	**R**	**Y**

C

2	4	5	1	3
P	**O**	**R**	**T**	**I**
S	**M**	**A**	**D**	**E**
I	**N**	**P**	**O**	**R**
T	**U**	**G**	**A**	**L**

D

2	4	5	1	3
B	**U**	**C**	**K**	**S**
F	**I**	**Z**	**Z**	**I**
S	**A**	**C**	**O**	**C**
K	**T**	**A**	**I**	**L**

E

2	4	5	1	3
G	**U**	**I**	**N**	**N**
E	**S**	**S**	**I**	**S**
G	**O**	**O**	**D**	**F**
O	**R**	**Y**	**O**	**U**

F

2	4	5	1	3
A	**N**	**I**	**P**	**I**
S	**A**	**Q**	**U**	**A**
R	**T**	**E**	**R**	**B**
O	**T**	**T**	**L**	**E**

G

2	4	5	1	3
C	O	G	N	A
C	I	S	A	B
E	T	T	E	R
D	R	I	N	K

H

2	4	5	1	3
C	H	A	N	G
E	D	W	A	T
E	R	I	N	T
O	W	I	N	E

The key cipher is

3	2	5	4	1

I

W	I	N	E	I
S	O	N	L	Y
S	W	E	E	T
T	O	H	A	P
P	Y	M	E	N

J

M	A	R	S	A
L	A	I	S	P
R	O	D	U	C
E	D	I	N	S
I	C	I	L	Y

K

K	I	R	R	O
Y	A	L	C	O
N	T	A	I	N
S	C	H	A	M
P	A	G	N	E

L

S	T	R	E	G
A	M	E	A	N
S	W	I	T	C
H	I	N	I	T
A	L	I	A	N

M

M	E	T	O	X
A	I	S	A	B
R	A	N	D	Y
F	R	O	M	M
E	X	I	C	O

N

T	O	N	I	C
W	A	T	E	R
C	O	N	T	A
I	N	S	Q	U
I	N	I	N	E

O

A	M	A	G	N
U	M	C	O	N
T	A	I	N	S
T	W	O	B	O
T	T	L	E	S

P

D	A	O	I	S
A	R	E	D	W
I	N	E	F	R
O	M	P	O	R
T	U	G	A	L

Brain Teasers

1 (a) PRINCIPAL CHAMPAGNE HOUSES
(b) BOLLINGER
(c) MOET AND CHANDON
(d) POL ROGER
(e) CHARLES HEIDSIECK
(f) LANSON
(g) KRUG
(h) G H MUMM
(I) LOUIS ROEDERER
(j) TATTINGER
(k) VEUVE-CLICQUOT
(l) LAURENT-PERRIER

2 (a) BANDOL (LANGUEDOC)
(b) TAVEL (RHÔNE)
(c)CHINON (LOIRE)
(d)BOURG (BORDEAUX)
(e)ANJOU (LOIRE)
(f)FLEURIE (BURGUNDY)
(g)FRONSAC (BORDEAUX)
(h)SAUTERNES (BORDEAUX)
(I)FITOU (CORBIERES)
(j)VOUGEOT (BURGUNDY)
(k)CORBIERES (LANGUEDOC)
(l)GIGONDAS (RHÔNE)

Crosswords

1 1 Bourgueil, 2 Armagnac, 3 Clicquot, 4 4 Rudesheim, 5 Burgundy
2. 1 Ouzo, 2 Mistral, 3 Krug, 4 Mirabelle, 5 Bourgueil
3. 1 Mersault, 2 Rheinhessen, 3 Grape, 4 Valais, 5 Galliano, 6 Manzanilla
4. 1 Benedictine, 2 Frascati, 3 Southern Comfort, 4 Van der Hum, 5 Burgundy
5. 1 Gamay, 2 Cognac, 3 Piedmont, 4 Loire, 5 Grand Marnier, 6 Amontillado
6. 1 Manhatten, 2 Pink Lady, 3 Rusty Nail, 4 Bailey's, 5 Paradise
7. 1 Barolo, 2 Semillon, 3 Valdepenas, 4 Gamay, 5 Maple Leaf.
8. 1 Bairrada, 2 Valdepenas, 3 Calvados, 4 Sercial, 5 Amontillado, 6 Manzanilla, 7 Valpolicella.
9. 1 Cassis, 2 Mirabelle, 3 Bronte, 4 Van der Hum, 5 Maraschino, 6 Chartreuse
10. 1 Strega, 2 Bronte, 3 Maraschino, 4 Provence, 5 Grenache.
11. 1 London Fog, 2 Sandalford, 3 Curacao, 4 Malaga, 5 Cointreau
12. 1 Chianti, 2 Tia Maria, 3 Gironde, 4 Napa Valley, 5 Noilly Prat, 6 Chardonnay
13. 1 Baileys, 2 Malibu, 3 White Lady, 4 Grand Slam, 5 Hermitage
14. 1 Hudson, 2 Gironde, 3 Moselle, 4 Garonne, 5 Dordogne
15. 1 Maraschino, 2 Barolo, 3 Grape, 4 Ouzo, 5 Montepulciano, 6 Chartreuse.

Map Match

France

St Péray	Rhône
St Estèphe	Bordeaux
Morey-St-Denis	Burgundy
Sancerre	Loire
Fitou	Midi
Gerwürztraminer	Alsace
Arbois	Jura
Bandol	Provence
Seyssel	Savoie
Cahors	South West

Italy

The Marches	9
Umbria	10
Sardinia	5
Tuscany	11
Venezia	14
Piedmont	17
Latium	8
Calabria	3
Lombardy	16
Campania	6
Sicily	4
Trentino-Alto-Adige	15
Emilia-Romagna	12
Basilicata	2
Veneto	13
Liguria	18
Ambruzzo	7
Apulia	1

Spain

Navarra	4
La Mancha	9
Jerez	1
Rioja	5
Penedês	6
Valdapeñas	10
Malaga	2
Montillo	3
Alicante	8
Valencia	7

Germany

Baden	7
Franken	8
Ahr	1
Rheinhessen	6
Rheinpflaz	10
Mosel-Saar-Ruwer	3
Rheingau	4
Nahe	5
Mittelrhein	2
Württemberg	9

Australia

Swan Valley	2
Stainthorpe	4
Hunter Valley	1
McClaren Vale	13
Gin Gin	14
Coonawarra	12
Yarra Valley	7
Mudgee	8
Goulburn Valley	10
Barossa Valley	9
Roma	3
Rutherglen	6
Margaret River	5
Geelong	11

New Zealand

Whangerai	11
Canterbury	1
Wellington	4
Hamilton	8
Aukland	3
Nelson	2
Bay of Plenty	5
Marlborough	12
Kumeu	13
Gisborne	6
Waimauku	9
Waikanae	10
Napier	7
Renwick	14

United States of America

Napa Valley	4
Finger Lakes	10
Walla Walla Valley	6
Martha's Vineyard	11
Sonoma County	3
Hudson River	9
Dundee Hills	12
Mendocina	5
Santa Clara	2
Stag's Leap District	14
Madera	15
Monterey	1
Santa Barbara County	13
Monticello	7
Lake Michigan	16

Wordsearch answers

CHAMPAGNE

```
V U C O B I R A M V O N T O N I P P U O B I A S O D U C H A R D O N N
P I O O Z J E R O B O W E O R C L A S O D F E R K M E D O A U O B X T
W A U Q C E B E R R M A G R U K R A M N B R P S A R B O U W U O B J F
P Z U C H A M P A G R H Z Y S N O D R A H C R G W V U C K O D Y R A C
Y S B R Q C H A M P A U E F R B D R E B E N N Z C H A R D O N N O D O
M A R K U O B O B O N E F R A C K I M E Y U P R A C K I A D O U R E J
G R U N P M A R Q K A U M E R Q M A G J M P R A M J R E B E C Y C H A
G A P M A H C P G A P M A H C D O N T O N I P I A C M A R Q T O N I P
I K C A R R C E B E R S U O B C P I N O T M M S A H E Q I K C A R K C
G A P M A H C N P I N O T M E U N I Y A M J S T A M U H O U O B K B R
V E N R A M O R A M B A U M E R H P I N W E H M A G N S C J T O N I P
E R Q M Z G A P M A H C G R A M G H C Y M A R M E S S A A E H R A H C
H I G A W C H A R D O N N X P I N O O B U E D W E H M A R Y B U U O B
N G K O N B R Z A Y D E U O B Z I O L B Z A U T W U K C H A N E Q H C
G V D B R C U V J O A G R A N D K A E D U A C I P A Q P V U C M R N U
A B V O X C U I S Z D O O C U A G X C H A R D O N N C R M N T O N I P
P I S R J K X A B A U M E R Q E F B O U X D O N O D P E A A D N A R G
M F L E P A G D M A G N R T O N I P U C H A E M A U K G U M U R E M U
A V B J Z E R C U V I R E B E C E H H Y C H A R D O N N I W D S N I P
H C A U F C H A R D O N N Y C U O A P J E R O B O P A S S E L N S A S
C L O N T O N I P W C H A R D R R E B R U R A C K I J R E B E A A G J
R V X A U C C U V Z A U B P W D C N G A M B C H A R D O N N J A C R J
A U I G V D O S A U P I N E O F M C R E I N U E M T O N I P P J E F G
B O R N V R E M U A X D Q N C U A Z G R A N D M A R Q P U O B M V U C
I P L I X N G A M N V H N X T U R B W A S O D G B O U B L B M E S S A
S A K K Z B O R E J N A X B O U U G A P M A H C H C U V O O R D F V O
E J E C J M A R B H Y K C H A R D O N N T C U V G R E M U G O V R A C
D O O A W A U L R A M P F V E G A U M E R K R A M P P I Z U D R A C K
D O E R M R B C B O U X M A R S A S S E M B L A Y H C V X V B O R E J
U O B L R I O N T O N I P F R E B E C N O B O R E J D U A U D O F S A
```

ASSEMBLAGE	AUBE	BOUZY	BRUT
CHARDONNAY	CHAMPAGNE	CUVÉE	DOSAGE
DOUX	GRANDMARQUE	JEROBOAM	MAGNUM
MARNE	PINOT MEUNIER	PINOT NOIR	RACKING
REBECHE	REMUAGE		

BURGUNDY

N E F R A C K I M E Y U P R A C K I S R O U R E J G R U N P M A

R Q K A U M E R Q B E A U J O L A I S M A G J M P R A M J R E B

E I R U E L F A P M A N C P G A L P E A H C D O N T O N I P I A

C M A R Q T O N I P I K U A R B C E S E R S U O N O G R O M T M

M S A H E Q I K C A R K C A A P M A I C N P I E O T J M U N I Y

A M J S T A M U H O U O B H E R T D A I D F V P B K M E N R A M

O R A M B A O M E R H P C N W B H M N G N A C J T A N I P E R Q

M Z G A P M N H C G R A M P A G R H N V N N O D R A H C R G W V

U C K O D Y T A C Y S B R Q C H A M O I U E F D B D E E B E N N

Z C H A R D R N N O D O M A R K U O L O B O N E F S A C K I M E

Y M M O N T A G N Y O U R E J G R U A P M A R Q I A U M E R Q M

A G J M P R C M J R E B E C Y C O A H A P M A A C P G A T M A H

C Y O N T O H I P I A C M A R M T O C I P I N C A R R M L H C Y

M A A M E S E A A E G R A H C E I G U W C N A R D O N N U P I N

O O B N E D T E B M I R Y B U U O B N G O O N B R Y A Y A E U O

B Z I O L B Z A U U V U K C H A N E Q L C G V D B R E U S J O A

G R A N D Q A E D U R C I P A Q P V A C M R N U A B V R R C U I

S Z D O O C V A G X Y G A R D O N H C R M N T O N I P P U S R J

K X A B A U M E R Q E F U O U X C O N O D P E A R D N A E C M F

B R O U I L L Y A G N R T O N I P U C H A E M A U K G U M M R U M

U A V B J Z E R C U V I R E D E C E H H Y C L A R D O N N I W M

S N I P H C A U F C H A R D K Y M D P J U L I E N A I S R M E P

E K U F W C A L N Y E F T W L P U M B G Y F O Y U R F N M S E X

Z K S A I A N N O C A M R S D L J N V X F E S Q K J I F B N P K

CHALONNAISE	MOULIN A VENT	BEAUJOLAIS
MONTRACHET	MACONNAIS	MEURSAULT
BURGUNDY	BROUILLY	MONTAGNY
JULIENAS	MERCUREY	POMMARD
CHABLIS	FLEURIE	VOLNAY
BEAUNE	MORGON	BEAUNE
RULLY	GIVRY	

BORDEAUX

M J P F L E P A L K M G I R X W E D J H Y F O L M J H G Y B F C D K
R F D F Y Y E G D M A G N R T O N I P U C H A E M A A K A U A U R E
M U A V B J T E L H F S E F C X N U O S R H B R O R M L M L N O T C
G E S W K U R B G L I T T K H L F K S T A O Q M O N O C L R X R E K
U B Y H P L U G D E A S N N P I R C U E I R E N E C E I H Y C H A R
D O N N I W S S N I P H O G U R D S E M V K N L F G U J H G T H I M
G T L O G D S E E S A U T E R N E S L I K E G F D A R E O P M V C D
G R S R E S E G T E A I I J K V B Z Q L H F R S P I U E R N V B H K
U T D L O J M B G U R O I O T D S E V I H T Y F R D S L I K N B V C
H T F K N L M U O R D G C S E A W W U O H Y N G V E L I X W E I H F
R K Y L O R E M O R W J P M F T B E S N N F J M C R A X P R T N F K
D Z V E Y W Q M B P D X I M Z E A D W J U G T M V L P G G D F E L Z
M P K U G D E A Q K P E B Y F R K D M B L S T J U L I E N V T G L C
R A G X U E H F M B K L A A Z D Q K I P O N G D R F R V C G P R S E
F X A J M B X H O P A W R U J O K M V G D A R L M A H V X Z R O L J
T D W P L M Y V R Y J H B T X C R H K U Y W Q B C N C K O G H K P Y
S P I B R F C E E X W F U M J D E Z G I Y W Q L K O F G I Y U E Y R
E K G O M B U D E A K J P R X Z E W M L H U T G D S R W Q M N I G C
H H K U I S K O L Y F R C G V D Y Q U E M R J G N U E U N T V Y Z U
P D S R E O E M V C D G R S R E S E G D E A I I J K V N Z Q I H F R
E F I G E R N V B H K U T D L O J M B N U R O I X T D S G V C H Y F
T D S L I K N B V A C H T F K N L M U T O D G C U E A W W U O T O N
S U C H A E M A U R G U M U R E H Y N R S E L I A W K I H F D K Y H
E M O T X R W J P M G T B E S K D T O I E P U C G A E M A U K R U M
T R E M U I V B J Z E L H F S E F R X G T O K R R B R O P M L M O N
S T C G E G W K U O C O D E M K H L O K S L A O A M E N O C I R X D
E K U B Y H P L P G D E A S N N F K V D N O T R M O G R V K U D F N

SAUTERNES
BORDEAUX
BERGERAC
GIRONDE
PETRUS
BLAYE

ST ESTÈPHE
PAUILLAC
DORDOGNE
GARONNE
GRAVES
MEDOC

ST ÉMILION
ST JULIEN
MARGAUX
POMEROL
D'YQUEM
BOURG

LOIRE

M F L E P R G D M A G N Q T O N I P U C H A E M A U K G U M U R E M
U A V B J Z U R C U V I R U B E C E H H Y C H A R D O N N I W R S N
I P H U Y H V M R D E S N J I G T Y F D R C E E O L M H U J I G F D
M R W S X G T W U Z L P Y U M N O I H N T G D M M L D U Y O W S R M
B U J H D U Y Z T A D O I M L R C S T O N I P U U H A E L A U K G U
M U S E M U A V B J S E L H F S E Y C X N U O K R F B R O P M L M H
N O T C G E S W K P O B G L I T T K H L F K S L A O Y M E N O C I R
X R E K A B Y H P O P G D E A S N N T O N I P U C H A L M A U K G U
M U R E M D A V B U Z E L H F S E F C X N U O K R H B R L P M T M H
N O T C G E E W K I O B G L I T T K H L F K S L A O Q M E I O C I R
X R E K U B Y T P L P G D E A S N N E J G K M G B F V S O U U I U N
G Y D R G T C S Z L C S E P L U M B J H U G Y R D K M V R H F O Y C
E X R K L S Z T E Y P K M B H T G R S E W J L K O G B A R V T U P Y
X L K P R D W N O S M Y J G H Y T D W S E V X J M P I U J Y F V T I
E X S F G E W K P U N B U G Y C B O U R G U E I L N I P H M B T F E
C W Z J Y B T M L R U J F R I U N T G Y N Y V T E T J U G N T B U G
O Y H G L M U B T L R W M A Y F P B T Y F Y Y H R D E L H F V R U B
N L P I F T W K B O E D W B N I T S X U L M I H Y T C D K U N T Y A
R W M V J G I Y H I E W B K P J R S R L B H F L U M N Y H B R F D E
A K V T C R V R H R S G N G Y D O J I F R H R F H R F B R H U J F R
H F O G T O N I P E I H A E M A U X G U M U R V M U A V B J E E L H
F S E F C X N U O K U H B R O P E L M H N O T C Q E S W K U R B G L
I T T N O N I H C L O O Q M E R O C I R X R E K U U Y H P L R G D E
A S N N R E S M J V L T V Y T L G J N T V F G F H P V I R G E E S Z
G U T E I M B L O J T D R W J P O M K H Y D E S T Q J R U M C T V R
X E D F H W K B T V N B F R G P T O N I P U C H A E M A A K N U M U
R E M U A V B J Z E O H F S E F C X N U O K R H B R O P M Y A H N O
T C G E S W K U O B M L I T T K H L F K S L A O Q M E N O C S R X H

POUILLY SUR LOIRE
BOURGUEIL
SANCERRE
QUINCY
LOIRE

POUILLY FUMÉ
MUSCADET
REUILLY
CHINON
ANJOU

MONTLOUIS
TOURAINE
VOUVRAY
SAUMUR

RHONE

M L E P P C D M Q A G N T R T O N I E P S C H F A E M A U F H K G N
M U R E X O U B G T D L K M U H N F R T S D C O I U R E M H L J U G
J D H T H T F E S W X R C W C R N Y P M I B U V Y C R X K R Z R W C
E V Y V R E G B Y M K O P U F O Y E O I U Y H U M U K N U E B T M U
C E Z W C B A F R S B U Y R M O R B Y N P L Y H I J U T F E J Y L P
J I M G U L E F S R T U B C G A W N K O L H Y D R M N I T Y F V E C
W X P K I O Y F I Y J B N L Y P T D A F T A V E L T F O S X K I N O
P M Y G B N T R C E S X Q O P K Y N J S K I M B H Y C J N M I T B R
B Y G V H D O F I M V J K O L I P K C U Y T R D R L N F T E W X F R
D S Q J O E N T Y R C E D F Y U P O L A T D C S G S L P D K W P R O
T C M K O U O F E W K H F V E D C L O K R J Y H P K M Y P N E J R E
F R L H G R H T F R B E A U M E D E V E N I S E V D E C W P X K I J
R F G Y E T J I K N M H B T U T G V E D C W L X T R U M A H Y G T M
K J Y T R R E N V V P L O M E T E D W C G F T I R W S P L P M K U Y
T F O T J E M D O G P C O E I A Y I J U E D N H F T U Y H T D F L U
J C T F R T O I I P U C H A R M U U K G U M U R E D U A V B J Z E L
H F S E F C X N T O K R H B D O P G L M H N O T N G E S W K U O H G
L I T T K H L F K A L A O Q N E N O R I R X R E K U B Y H P L P P D
E A S N N W S X J I G N R F O H L O D I T S T Q L K M N Y J M I E Y
R E W S X D C F V G B E N J C K O J I G L A F R D E S W A Q L P S J
N S A D N O G I G X A Z Z S X D C F V E H L B T N Y M U P U M H O Y
T R G V R G V R G J I L K U M H B T V C N Y E R M E M U G T E C J B
U R E I M J N Y E C W Z M K I F W V T G N U G T R E W L M I N Y T A
V B J Z E R C U V I R E B E C E H H Y C H A R D O N N I W D S N S P

BEAUME DE VENISE
CÔTE BLONDE
CÔTE BRUNE
ST JOSEPH
LIRAC

CHÂTEAU GRILLET
CÔTE ROTIE
GIGONDAS
ST PÉRAY
TAVEL

HERMITAGE
CONDRIEU
CORNAS

GERMANY

```
M L E P P G D F Q A G N T R T O S S O L H C S F A E M A U F H K G U R
U R E X I U B G R D L K M U H N F R T S D C O I U R E M H L J K G E D
H T H R F E S W X A C W B R N Y O M I B U V Y C R X R Z E W C I V Y
V R V G B Y M K O P N F T Y G O I U Y H U M U K N U E B T M U N E Z W
C E A F R S B U Y R M C J B Y N P L Y H I J E T F R J Y L P P I M G U
V E F S R T U B N G T W O K O L H Y D R M H I H Y F V E C F X P K I M
Y F I Y J B N L K I T D R N W R U B V T A R S X K M N O A M Y G B H T
R C E S X Q O P K Y E J L K I M B H Y N J N M I T O R L Y U V H I O F
R H E I N G A U P K I W Y E R A R L N F T E W X F S Z Y N R S V H L O
D V T S W Q L K M N Y Y S M I G L U M N H Y B A D E N Y G R D L N V V
P L O M J T E D W C G L T I R W S X L P M K U Y T L R T J E L D E G P
C O E F V Y I S U E I N H F E B Y H T D F L U J B T F R W S X J I S N
E F V H L O P V T N W Q L K M N X B U M J N Y R D H R W H O I M H B E
L B K I G A E Y G M N H Y G T M K J Y G R D E N V V P L O M J T E D A
U G F T T R W S X L P M K R Y T F R T J E L D O G P C O E F V Y I J H
A D N L F T B Y H T D F L O J B T F R W S X J I Y N R R D S N J O I R
F Y E C E D F Y U P O L N T D C S G S L P R H E I N H E S S E N D K W
L S O T C M K K U R F E W W J F V E D C L O K I J Y H P K M K P N U J
E E F R L T G N A T F R V E E C W S X K I J R F G Y H T J I C N M H B
D V T G V E D C W B X T R I M N H Y G T M K J Y G R D E N V O P L O M
E T E D W C G F T I I W S N L P G K U Y T F R T J E L D O G R C O E F
V Y I J U E D N H F T N Y H T I F L U J B T F R W S X J I Y T R F V H
L O D V T S W Q L K M N E J Z I U Y R E W S T K E S V G B H N J M K O
J I G U T F R D E S W A Q T P M J N H B G V F C D S M A Z Z S X D C F
V E V R B T N Y M U P U I H T Y T R G V R G V R G J I R K U M H B T V
R N Y C R M E M U G T R C F B U R E I M J N Y E C W Z M O I F W V T G
N U G Y R E W L M I P Y Y V A V B J Z E R C U V I R E B E C W H H Y C H
A R D O N N I W D S N D P L F G I K G U N F P C W V R P L J G F S G M
```

RHEINHESSEN
FRANCONIA
RIESLING
ROTWEIN
TROCKEN
WORMS
SEKT

RHEINPFALZ
KABINETT
SPRITZIG
EISWEIN
SCHLOSS
MOSEL
AHR

EDELFAULE
RHEINGAU
SPATLESE
AUSLESE
BADEN
NAHE

SPAIN/PORTUGAL

U M N H Y G T M K J Y G R D E N V V P L O A D A N A W C G F T I R W

S X A P M K U Y T F R T J E L D O G P C O E F V R I J U E D N H R T

B Y H R D F L U J B T J E L D O G P C O E F V E I J U E D N H A T B

Y H T D S L U J B T F R W S X J I Y N R F V L L O D V T S W Y L K M

N Y Y F M A G L U M N H Y G T M K J Y G R O E N V V P L R A Y T F R

T J E L D O L P C O E F V Y I J U E D N S F T B Y H T D F L U J B T

F R W S X J I A N R F V H L O D V T S W Q H K M N Y U M NO M J T E

D W C G F T I R W S X L P T M U Y T F R T J E L D O G P C O E F V Y

I J U E D N H F T B Y H T D A L U J B T F R W R X J I Y N R F V H L

O D V T S W Q L K M N X B U D W N Y R D H R W H R I M H A G A L A M

G X E Y U M N H Y G T M F R E S N J I Y N R F V H Y O D V T S W Q L

K M N Y U M N H Y G T M K J I G R Y E N V V P L S M J T E D W C G F

T I R W S R M N P T I E B T R C R W S L O H B A P Y M R N W C U J Y

V X L P M K U Y T F R T J E A D O G P C O E T V Y I J U E D N H F T

B Y H T D A L U J B T F R W S X J I Y N R N V H L O D V T S W Q L K

M N Y U M N N Y G T M K J Y G R D E N V I P L O M J T E D W C G F T

I R W S X L P Z K U Y T F R T K J Y G U D E N V V P L O M J T E D W

C G F T I R W S A L P M K H Y G T M Q J Y G R D E N V V P L O M J T

E D W C G F T I R W S X L P M K U Y T F R T J E L D O G P C O E F T

Y I J U E D N H F T B Y H T A F L U J B T S R W S X J I Y N R F V R

L O D V T S W Q L K M N Y R M N M K U Y T E R T F L O R O G P C O O

F V Y I J U E D N H F T B Y H T D F L U J R T F R W S X J I Y N R P

V H L O D V T S W Q L D M N Y P H R S E W C V D E N V V P L O M J T

E D W C G F T I R W A R M N P T I E B T D I H Y G T M K J Y G R D E

N V V P L O M J T L D W C G F T I R W S X A P R W S L O H B D P Y M

R N W C U J Y V R L P M K U Y T F R T J E L D O G P C O E F V Y I J

U O D N H F T C Y H T D F L U J B T F R W S X J P A L O M I N O O D

V L S W Q L K M N Y U M N H Y G T M K J Y G R D E A V V P L O M J T

E O W C G F T I R W S X L P M K U Y A F U T S E L D G G P C O E F V

Y R J U E D N H F T B Y H T D F L U J B T F R W S X J E Y N R F V H

L O D V T S W Q L K M N Y Y F MI G L U M N H Y G T M K D Y G R D E

N S V P L O M J T E D W C G F T I R W S X L P M K U Y T F O T J E L

D O G P C O E F V Y I J U E D N H F T B Y H T D F L U J B T B R W Y

MANZANILLA	PALOMINO	CRIADERA
QUINTAS	OLOROSO	SERCIAL
MADEIRA	MARSALA	ESTUFA
MALAGA	SOLERA	SHERRY
BODEGA	TAWNY	ANADA
FLOR	PORT	RAYA

ITALY

```
U M N H Y G T M K J Y G R D E S V V P L O M J T E D W P G F T
I A W S X L P M O N I L O D R A B L D O G P I T N A I H C J U
E R N H F T B Y H T D F L U J S T F R W S X J I Y E R F V H L
O S V T S W Q L K M N Y U M N S Y G T M K J Y G M D E N V V P
L A M J T E D W C G F T I R W I X L P M K U Y O F R T J E L D
O L P C O E F V Y I J U E D N C F T B Y H T N F R U J B T F R
B A R O L O N R F V H L O D V A S W Q L V T N Y W V P W U Q J
M O Q U M V U F R E I S A N H I G T M K E Y G R D E I V V P L
O M J T E D W C G S T I O W S A L P M K N Y T F R T J E L D O
G P C O E F V Y I T U E D A H F T B Y H A D F L U J B T T R W
S X J I Y N R F V E L O D V V S W Q L K C N Y V S E M P O O U
Y B H Y N T V R V S K D L U Y E M N H Y C T M K J Y G R D E N
V V P L O M J T E T W C G A T I R W S X I P M K U Y T F I T J
E L D O G P C O E E V Y L J M E D N H F A O Y H T D F T U O B
O F R W S X J I Y S R L V H L B D V T S W Q C C K M A Y T T B
F I S E W M N L O T E J N R X W R Z J U K U M N S C G T M T J
Y G H D E N V V P C O M J T E D W U G F T I R W S E L P M E U
Y T F C T J E L I O G P C O E F V Y S J U E D A H F R B Y C T
D F L U C B T L R W S X J I Y N R F V C L O R V T S W A L L M
N Y U M N I O G T M K J Y G R D E N V V O F O M J T E D B O G
F T I R W P D L P M K U Y T F R T J E L D O G P C O E F V D I
J U E D L H F R B Y H T D F L U J B T F R W S X J I Y N R F A
H L O A V T S W E L A S T I S P U M A N T E K M N Y V Y T G B
J H V E Z W D E L V N Y G R F D K I J U N T M V U R T R W E C
```

ASTI SPUMANTE	VALPOLICELLA	VERTDICCHIO
BARBARESCO	LAMBRUSCO	BARDOLINO
EST EST EST	SASSICAIA	VERNACCIA
PIEMONTE	FRASCATI	DOLCETTO
CHIANTI	MARSALA	ORVIETO
FREISA	BAROLO	SOAVE

EUROPE

U M C H Y G T M K J Y G R D E N V V P L O M J T E D W C G F T I R
W S O L P M K U Y T F R T J E L D O G P O B E F V Y I J U E D N H
F T D Y H T D F L U J B T F R W S X J S Y N E F V H L O D V T S W
Q L E M N YU M T I K V R N H Y G T C K J Y G Y D E N V V P L O M
J T M D W C G F T I A I N O L A T A C Y T F R T C E L D O G P C O
E F V Y I J U E D N H F T B Y H T D F L U J B T F H W S X J I Y N
R F V H L O D V T S W Q L K V O E S X M N Y U M N H E G T M K J Y
G S T T U P V P L O M J T E D W C G F M I K W S X L P V K U Y T F
R T J E L D O G P C O C F V Y I J U E D A H F T B Y H T E F L U J
B T F A L B A R I N O O F V H L O D V B S R Q L K M N Y V L Y G M
N H Y G T M K J Y G R N E N V V P L I M J T C D W C G F I I L R S
X L P M K U Y T F R T D E L D O G N C O E F V H I J U E O N H E T
B Y H T D F L U J B T R R W S X E I Y N R F V H E O D V G S W B L
K M N Y U M N H Y G T I K J Y T R D E N V V P L O M J T N D W S G
F T I R W S X L P M K E Y T T Y R T J E L D O G P C O E F I Y I S U
E D N H T T B Y H T D U L U J B T F R W S X J I Y N R F E H L O D
V T S W Q O E M N YU M N H Y G T M K J Y G R D E N V V R L O L J
T E D W C G K I I R W S X L P M K U Y T F R C J E L D O G P C H E
F V Y I A U E A R H F T B Y H T D F L U J H T F R W S X J I Y C R
F V H L I D V N Y U R M N U C F R S W C A S W Q L K M N Y U M S H
Y G T M V J Y G R D E N V V P L O M J B E D W C G F T G R W S X L
P M K U A T F R T J E L D O G P C O L F V Y I J U E D N R F M B Y
H T D F D U J B T F R W F X J A N I S T E R L O D V T S W A L K M
N Y U M L H Y G T M K J Y G R D S N V V P L O M J T E D C C V F T
I R W S O L P M K U Y T F R T J E L D O G P C O E F V O I J U E D
N H F T M Y H T D F L U J B T F R W S X J I Y N R F N H L O D V S

BEYCHEVELLE	SCHLOSSBERG	CATALONIA
KABINETT	ALBARINO	VIOGNIER
MOLDAVIA	CONDRIEU	CHABLIS
FLEURIE	MOSCATO	RETSINA
MARCHE	GRAVES	MACON
MEDOC	TOKAY	PUTTS

LIQUEURS

U M N H Y G T M K J Y G R G E N V V P L O M J T E D W C C F T I

R W S X L P M K U Y T F R A J E L D O G P C O E F V Y U J U E D

N H F T B Y H T D F L U J L T F R W S X J I Y N R F R H L O D V

T S W Q L K M N Y D T I R L S X W S X L P G K U Y A F R T J E L

D O G P C O E F V Y I J U I D N H F S X J I L N C F V H L O S V

P Y B T D R E C M N B Y B A S W Q L K M N T I A W S X L P I K U

Y T F R T J E L D O G P C N E F V S I J U E O N Y F T B S H T D

F L U J A T F R W S X J I O N R F V Y L O D V T S V Q S K M N Y

B E N E D I C T I N E G R D E N V V P E O M J T E D A B Y H T D

F L U J Y T F R W S X J I Y N R F V H L L D V N U C R M N U C F

R S W C O S W Q L K M N K U M N H Y G T M I J U G R D E N V V P

L O M J C E D W C G F U I R W S X L P M K U A T F R T J E L D O

G P C O A F V Y I J M T D N H F T B Y H T E F B U J B T F R W S

X J I Y A R F V H M O D R T S W Q L K M R Y U M N H Y G T M K J

Y G R D T N V V E L O M J O E D W C G T T I R W S X L A M K U Y

T F R T J E L L O G P C O E F V Y I N U E D N H F T B Y I T D F

L U J B T F R W W C G F T I R M S I L P B K U Y T F R T J H L D

O G P C O E F V Y I J U E D N H O T B Y R T D F L U J B T F A W

S X J I Y N R F V H L O D V N C F C M N O C F R S W C T S W Q B

K M N Y U M N H Y G T M K J Y G R D N N N V P L O M J T E D W C

G F T I K W S X L P M K U Y T F R T J R T D O G P C O E F V Y I

J U E D N A F T B Y H T D F L U J B T F E W S X J I Y N R F V H

L O D V T S H Q L K M N Y U U N H Y G T M H J Y G R D E N V V P

L O M J T E D L C G F T I R B S X L P M K L T M K U Y T F R T J

E L D O G P C O U F V Y I J I E D N H F T B Y U T D F L U J B T

F R W S X J I Y N A F V H L L D V T S W Q L K M O Y U M N H Y G

T M K J Y G R D E N V V P L A M J T E D W C G F T S R U Y T F R

T J E L D O G P C O E F V Y M J U E D N H F T B Y H T D F L U J

B T F R W S X J I R E I N R A M D N A R G B T D R E C M N B Y B

SOUTHERN COMFORT	GRANDMARNIER	BENEDICTINE
COINTREAU	GALLIANO	ADVOCAAT
BAILEYS	CURACAO	KAHLUA
KUMMEL	GLAYVA	MALIBU
BRONTE	CASSIS	BAHIA

COCKTAILS

L P M K U Y T F R T J E L D O G P C O E F V Y I J U E B N H

F T B Y H T D F L U J B M A P L E L E A F N R F V H R O D V

H U F R M N U C F R S W C I S W Q L K F N Y U M N O Y G T M

K A Y G R D E N V V P L O Q J T E D I C G F T I N W S X L P

M K R Y T F R T J E L D O U P C O R F V Y I J X E D N H F T

B Y H V D F L U J B T F R I S X S I Y N R F V H L O D V T S

W Q L K E N Y U M N H Y G R M T J R G R D E N V V P L O M J

T E D W G Y F T I R W S X I N M K U E T N N O O M Y E N O H

C O E F V O W J U E D N L I M K U Y T Y R E J E L D P G P C

O E F V Y I F A E D N H G T B Y H T D F A U T B T A R W S X

J I Y N R F V N L O D H T S W Q L K M N Y R M T R Y G T M K

J Y G R D E N V O L T O M J T E D W C G F T P A A F T B Y H

T D F L U J B T F D B S X J I Y N R Y V H L D S V H Y B T D

R E C M N B Y B T S N A L K M N T D R W S I L P N K N Y T F

R T J E L D O G P C O O N V Y I A U E D S H F T B E H A D F

L U J B T F R W S X J I L G R L V H L E D V T S W Q D K M N

Y U M N H Y G T M K J Y G R E E N V V P L L M J T E D I C G

F M I R W S X L P M K U Y T F R T J E L D I G P C O E F A Y

I J A E D N H F T B Y H I D F L Y J B T F A W S X J I Y N M

F V H L O D V N U F R H N U C F D S W C T N W Q L K M N Y U

M N H Y S T M K J Y W R D E N V A P L O M Y T E D W C G F T

I R W S X D P M K U Y T F R T J L L D O G T C O E F V Y I J

U E D N H F N B Y H T D F L U J K T F R W S N Y L K O O R B

H L O D V T S A Q L K M N Y U M N H Y G T U K J Y G R D E N

V V P L O M J T R D W C G F T I I W S X L R M K U Y T F R T

J E L D O G P C O G B T D E M L P K K H I F O C E B I O N T

HARVEY WALL BANGER
WHITE LADY
HONEYMOON
MANHATTEN
DAIQUIRI

MAIDENS PRAYER
MAPLE LEAF
GRAND SLAM
PINK LADY .
BROOKLYN

FIRST NIGHT
LONDON FOG
RUSTY NAIL
PARADISE
BRONX

MINERAL WATERS

L P M K U A T F R T J E L D O G P C O E F V Y B J U E D N H F T M
Y H T D N L U J B T F R W S X J I Y N R F V H U O D V N U F R A N
U C F N S W C T S W Q L K M N Y U M N H Y G T X K J Y G R D L N V
V P A O M J T E D W C G F T I R W S X L P M K T Y T F R T V E L D
O P P S O E F V Y A P P O L I N A R I S I J U O D N H F E B Y H T
D F L U H B T F R W S X J I Y N R F V H L O D N T S W R L K M N Y
U M N H Y B T M K J Y G R D E N V V P L O M J T A D N C G F T I R
W S X L P M O U Y T F R T J E L D O G P C O E F V G I J U E D N H
F T B Y H T D U L U J B T F R W S X J I Y N R F V H O O D V P Y B
T D R E C M N B R B T S W Q L K M N T I R W S X L P M W U Y T F R
T J E L D O G P C N E F V Y I J U E D N H V T B Y H T D Y L U J B
T F R W S X J I Y N E F V H L O D V T S W I L K M N Y U M L H Y G
T M K J Y G R D E N V V P L O M J T E D W T G F T I R W S X L P M
K U Y T F R T J E L O O G P C O C F V Y I T U E D N H F T B Y A T
D F L U J B T F R W L X J I Y N R O V H L E D V N U F R M N U C B
R S W C T S W Q L K V N Y U M N H Y N T M L F Y G R T E N V V P L
O M J T E D W C G F I I R W S X L P M T U A T F R T I E L D O G P
C O E F V Y I J U E C N H F T B Y H T D R L U J B T O R W S X J I
Y N R F V H L O A V T S W Q L K M N Y R M E H Y G T D K J Y G R D
P E R R I E R M J L E D W C G F T I A W S X X P M K A Y T F R T J
E L D O G P C O W S L J I Y N R F R H L O D V N U F B M N U C F R
S W C T S W Q L K M N E U M N H E G T M K J Y G R D E N V V P L O
M J T E D W C G F T I R V S X L P M K U Y T F R T J E L N A I V E
O E F V Y I J U E D N H F T L Y H T D F L U J B T F R W S X J I Y
N R F V H L O D V T S W Q E N M N Y Y M N H Y G T W O R S C J U M
L P E W Q X F R M N B O I T M O J Y G R D E N V V P L O M J T E D
W C G F T I R W S X L P M K U Y F F R T J E L D O G P C O S P A H

APPOLLINARIS
ASHBOURNE
MALVERN
VITTEL
EVIAN

FERRARELLE
FONTVELLA
PERRIER
BUXTON
PANNA

BALLYGOWAN
CONTREX
VOLVIC
BADOIT
SPA

GLOSSARY

ASSEMBLAGE	The blending of wines of the same origin
AUTOVINIFACTOR	A closed vat
BONNE CHAUFFE	An immature or infant cognac which is matured in barrels to colour and mellow
BROUILLIS	The pure clear spirit obtained during distillation. This is the coeur or the heart of the distillation which is redistilled to form an immature cognac also known as Bonne Chauffe.
TETE (HEADS)	The milky product run off until the spirit turns clear (Brouillis) until the spirit turns milky again (Queue-Tails) both of these milky liquids are distilled again. (In Scotland the heart head and tails are called 'low wines', 'foreshots' and 'feints' in the distillation of whisky.)
DEBOURAGE	The must (wine juice) is cleansed in a tank with sulphur dioxide for 24 hours after which the solid matter in the liquid is removed.
DEGORGEMENT	Removal of the sediment produced by the second fermentation in a champagne bottle.
D.O.C.	Corresponding to French A.O.C. and German Q.b.A.
D.O.C.G.	Highest grade with a government seal of quality.
DOSAGE	(Liqueur d' Expedition) A sugared wine added to bottles of sparkling wines prior to corking.
DUNDAR	A thick dark caramelised residue left in rum making. Can be used to make sour mash whiskey.
EAU DE VIE	A fruit brandy in which the sugar of a fruit has been used in the fermentation and distillation.
GUYOT SIMPLE	Methods of vine training, growth is double gathered into one or two stems.
GYROPALETTES	A machine used to remuage 500 bottles of champagne in one week compared to 4 weeks if remuage is carried out by hand.
HIGH ESTER	Heaviest style of all rums.
LEES	The sediment deposited by young wines in barrels or vats consisting mainly of dead yeasts.
MATURE	Ready to drink
MISTELLE	Unfermented grape juice which has alcohol added to it.
MUST	Juice from grapes before it has been fermented into wine.
PUPITRES	Special shaped hinged boards with angled holes to facilitate remuage by hand.

RACKING	Periodic decanting of wines from one barrel to another to separate it from the lees.
REBECHE	The juice obtained from the final pressing is used for local drinking or made into a fiery spirit called 'marc'
REMUAGE	In order to remove sediment in champagne bottles it has to be moved to the neck of the bottle. This is achieved by riddling a process of twisting each bottle a little each day in special shaped boards. This takes about 4 weeks and the skilled operators are known as remueurs. (See also Gyropalettes.)
SUR-POINTES	Vertical storage of bottles neck down at completion of remuage.
TANNIN	A substance found in the skins and pips of grapes and acts as a preservative. Similar to stewed tea it accounts for the puckering effect in young red wines.
UNA RAYAS	A fuller must without flor. Used for Oloroso.
DOS RAYAS	Inclined to be coarse and not so good.
RAYA PUNTO	The must has an excess of acidity and not clean and is used for distillation.
VENDAGE	Harvest
VIN DE CUVÉE	The first 2000 litres of juice extracted from the first pressing and is top quality (champagne) cuvée can also mean the blending of wines.
VIN DE TAVOLA	Means table wine corresponding to Vin de Table (France) Taffelwein (Germany)